Lear

The Shakespeare Company

plays Lear at Babylon

Lear

The Shakespeare Company plays Lear at Babylon

Mike Johnson

99% Press
an imprint of Lasavia Publishing Ltd.
Auckland, New Zealand

www.lasaviapublishing.com

This edition published, 2018
First published by Hard Echo Press, 1986

Copyright © Mike Johnson, 1986
Cover design © Jennifer Rackham, Daniela Gast 2018
Mike Johnson logo image © Joanna Smith & Jennifer Rackham, 2018

This book is copyright. Apart from any fair dealing for the purpose of private study, research, criticism or reviews, as permitted under the Copyright Act, no part may be reproduced by any process without the permission of the publishers.

ISBN: 978-0-9941015-0-1

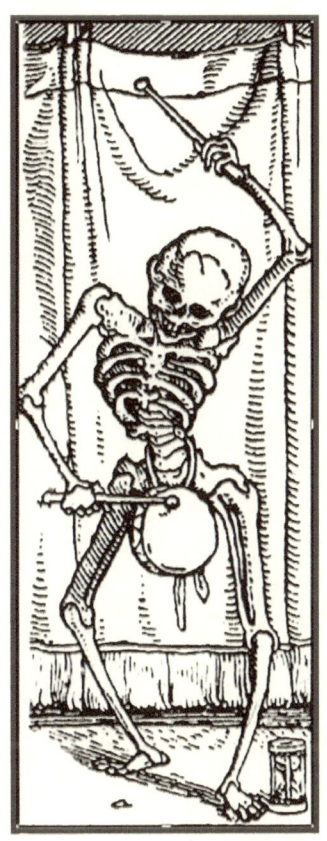

Death Drummer by Hans Holbein

Preface to the 2018 edition

Thirty-three years ago *Lear* was written, in about nine weeks, on a 1984 Sharp electric typewriter that was so noisy it shook the whole house. It was my first novel.

A year later, in 1986, *Lear* was published by Warwick Jordan of Hard Echo Press using an antique, 1902, C4 Intertype, Chandler and Price hand fed treadle platen and 'a very cranky Thompson Platen'. This machine had more moving parts than a steam engine, including a pot of boiling lead that would periodically explode. The book was held together by massive industrial staples making it not only durable but something of a 'postmodern artifact', an object out of the future the book portrays. There are still a few of this original edition around, but they are rare, and essentially the book has been out of print since the year it was published.

The novel had a impact when it came out, was widely reviewed and was shortlisted for the NZ Book Awards. Even now, all these years later, people will say, 'Oh, you're the guy who wrote *Lear*.' Another reader commenting recently said the book had not aged, that it could have been written now.

In preparing this edition, which had to be painstakingly retyped from the Hard Echo Press edition, I have retained the original text unmolested by my older self. I have kept everything, even some odd punctuation I would do differently now. Fidelity to the original has been my touchstone.

I'm proud to see this book finally republished in this handsome new edition, and wish it well in the modern marketplace, where, who knows, it might gain some new adherents.

Mike Johnson, Waiheke Island, December 2017.

The Blind Man by Hans Holbein

abylon!

Not the city of gleaming spires Lear wraps in silk; a black book falling open at endless markets, winding streets, curving arcades with silver and ormolu roofs sailing eternally against blue. A blue so intense it makes the eye shiver.

Towers and ziggurats rising slender from deserts; gardens shimmering with magnolias, cyclamen and roses. Archipelagoes of jade and amethyst over still water, measured by pyrographed domes and bronze statues. Air filled with the incense of sandalwood and attar, lavender and patchouli.

And people! This hard earth has not seen so many people. A great sinful press, awaiting the vengeance of the Lord.

They come in a sinuous weave of fragrance and colour, through the gardens and the shimmering heat. Lear throws his head back. Breathes deep. That a player should encompass such an audience! To your places!

Kings, caliphs, patricians, dukes, barons, their sweeping coats and their fine ladies. A slim ankle clasped in gold glimpsed behind the tapestry of a chrysophrase encrusted palanquin; the rich dark skin of a merchant from the fabled east; a silk robe with silver passementerie; the flash of an agate brooch worn by a queen's favourite. A procession in arabesque, winding through the twilit terraces where the first turquoise chalices are being raised. A princess, eyes the colour of coral, adjusts her ruby bracelet. Dark wine flows onto the tiles. A murmur ripples through the crowd. Backstage the players are quiet.

The mellow sound of a gong.

At least that's the way Lear would have it, squinting through the curtain at the crowd, a three-tiered auditorium hung in satin.

After the performance goats are slaughtered in the ritual fashion to the scream of parakeets and there is feasting well into the night. Naked slaves are offered the players with the most courteous of gestures. Tall, thin-legged birds pick their way fastidiously among the guests. There is quiet, ironical talk on the folly of old kings who divide their kingdoms; and coarse jokes at the folly of old men who whore their daughters. Toasts and accolades, punctuated by discreet bursts of laughter.

Curan, holding herself very still, shy as ever, hardly daring to breathe, eyes the young man with glossy black hair and lustrous skin who is pretending not to notice. Her hands begin to shake as amphorae filled with spicy, smouldering hashish are placed between vases of orchids. She tries to concentrate on the song Goneril is playing on the lute nearby, singing to two young women who kneel in front of her and look up at her rapturously.

In the garden, there is no match to the evening's perfection. See the moon flower with the peach blossom. In the arbour, Regan shakes out her hair. Ravens flicker past the torches.

Lear stands for a belated encore speech amid insistent clapping. He chooses one from near the end of the play when the major passions have run their course, lines in which anger and bitterness have smoothed into a grim and prophetic calm. It is a speech which offers precise scope for his baritone vibrato:

"Upon such sacrifices, my Cordelia,
The gods themselves throw incense. Have I caught thee?
He that parts us shall bring a brand from heaven,
And fire us hence like foxes. Wipe thine eyes;
The good years shall devour them, flesh and fell,
Ere they make us weep, we'll see 'em starve first."

He delivers these lines to Cordelia who smiles at him over the rim of her glass, the glass touching her teeth, the wine flashing a red depth. In the applause somebody throws a rose which lands on Curan's lap; white tinged with pink. Gloucester does not clap but watches with shattered, nervous eyes. The Fool is whispering something into his ear.

Lear sits down, face flushed, and lifts a piece of braised pork to his lips. Curan hides her face behind a fan.

Overhead, the sparkling Pleiades, a necklace of jewels buried, intact, in the black of night. Lights of another city.

Not our Babylon. A huddle of huts by the river. A filthy main street that leads to nowhere. Shacks that lean in on themselves. Low hills covered by a spiny forest overhung by a perpetual raft of dark cloud. A few urchin faces peering from doorways, the blotchy white of the Sickness on their limbs. And, low over the water, the mantric moan of the dying.

A straggling corn crop, hedged in by the mutant forest. The eye paints leaves with ridged backbones; trees dripping poisonous yellow sap;

cornstalks strangled by muscular vines; trunks that bend over and grow back towards the ground.

Two dirty yellow dogs dragging their haunches along the ground, heading for the jetty and our barge, *The Earl of Southampton*, nosing its way in.

"We're not going to stop here," Gloucester informs Edgar. Edgar is staring at the forest, his arms hugging his shoulders.

"What does it matter to you where you perform?" he replies, not looking at Gloucester. He appears to be hugging someone invisible. The two men are on deck, standing in the shadow of the wheelhouse. "What makes you so sure we're not stopping here?"

"Oh," Gloucester gives all the appearance of not wanting to state the obvious. "We've played here before."

But Lear says it will be all right, fixing the bright opal brooch on his coat, standing tall, *every inch a king*, long grey hair coming down past his shoulders.

"We've played in worse places than Babylon," he tells them. "Yes indeed. Every shitty town this side of the darkness. Why not Babylon? Bring a little light. A little fire to the ice, damn their eyes. Singe their beards and pluck out their hairs. Cover them with kisses. These shackers don't know they're alive."

Most of us are below deck, getting ready to disembark and listening to Lear. The candle wavers in front of the mirror as he turns his head from side to side, the shadows shifting with the line of his cheekbones. Even here, he tells them, a stage is still a stage. An audience an audience.

He buttons his doublet of royal purple, carefully sewn for him by Cordelia, and adjusts his crotch inside his baggy trousers. Wherever they go the magic of the Bard goes with them. Has the Bard ever let them down? He eases his cock gently into its codpiece. Cornwall and Albany snicker and elbow each other in the ribs.

"There must be at least fifty people in a place like this. Each one of them, no matter how humble or straitened his circumstances, will find something for the players. That adds up to a feast. The loaves and fishes principle."

He is addressing the mirror rather than the cast, trying to glimpse his own profile by swiveling his eyes as hard as he can to one side. Rewarded by tantalising glimpses.

Fifty people. Multiply that by fifty Babylons, that's a living. Fifty by fifty sad denizens who will pay to be, for some brief time, kings in their suffering and noble in their dying.

"Perhaps they'll kill us a pig," he says to Edmund over his shoulder, opening his eyes wide to the mirrored king. This facial contortion is a good trick to simulate astonishment or grief.

The Fool is watching Lear, his mouth hanging open idiotically. He shambles over to the king, and says,

"*She that's a maid now,*" a long pause as, moronically, he searches for the lines, "*Shall not be a maid long, unless things be cut shorter.*"

"Didn't I see a pig running around here, in that corn?" Lear says to Edmund, ignoring the Fool and tearing himself away from the mirror to nod and wink at the sly villain; the brawny grinning villain whose open necked shirt is embroidered with lace. Royalty can taste the fat on its lips, the slippery flesh between its teeth.

Edmund curtsies ingratiatingly.

The Fool taps Lear on the shoulder, and says in a low, conspiratorial tone,

"*If you should see Cordelia –
As no doubt you shall – show her this ring,*"

He points to the wooden stocks being unpacked from the hold with the rest of the props,

"*And she will tell you who your fellow is
That yet you do not know.*"

Brushing the Fool aside, Lear sits down to pull on boots of faded plastic. Finally, standing again, the crown, placed carefully askew with all the suggestion of slipping authority. The petulant quiver of the lower lip. This crown, flickering dully in the light, is made of real pewter. A gift from a royal patron who one night found tears coursing hotly down his cheeks; he who had not cried since the world had gone barbarous. He was very grateful for those tears and had presented Lear with the crown in honour of them.

His cloak of coarse Moroccan goat hair is pinned by a brooch of real opal. Nothing but genuine hydrous silica, we'll have you know, pellucid, but exhibiting a delicate play of colour; catching even the feeble candle light and throwing it.

Another quick look in the mirror. Perfect. Lear, you old fool. *Every inch a king*. A last minute adjustment to cloak and breeches; wrinkles out of the hose. The Lords and Ladies of Babylon are waiting!

Wait 'til the ignorant shackers see him in this garb. They'll come to the show all right, each bearing some little treasure for payment. Bless you, sir. Madam. There is no lack of treasures in this world, he tells the cast. Stolen from corpses, from empty houses where the Sickness has passed. Given the circumstances, can any of them say pickings have been lean?

Another wink to Edmund who nods, yes, yes indeed, and grinning fixedly, passes the wink on to Dukes Cornwall and Albany who pass it back and forth between them.

"*This is not Lear*," the Fool says to Edmund.

Lear polishes his brooch until it gleams in the candlelight, then with royal dignity ascends the stairs to the deck. His passage is marred only by some unpleasantness from the Fool who shouts after him angrily,

"*You owe me no subscriptions: then, let fall*
Your horrible pleasure; here I stand, your slave."

But Lear is already on the deck, waiting for Edgar to moor her, glancing up at the wheelhouse to Regan, who is bringing her in, and back to the jetty.

"What kind of place is this?" Gloucester asks, him standing by the railing, his face as grey as if caked with river mud or the residue of make-up.

Lear is off the barge and onto the rotting planking, shouting hoarsely, *"Blow winds, and crack your cheeks! rage! blow!*
You cataracts and hurricanes, spout
Till you have drenched our steeples, drown'd the cocks!
You sulphurous and thought executing fires ... "

No curious onlookers, the usual collection, sometimes a whole village, drawn to watch the *Earl of Southampton* dock and the players disembark. Always children, two or three, turning up from nowhere. Here Lear declaims to two drugged looking dogs and the village idiot who nods and drips saliva and giggles, staring at something to Lear's left.

"And thou, all shaking thunder,
Strike flat the thick rotundity of the world."

He spreads his hands to the sullen overcast sky, face twisted in grief. Goneril sighs tiredly. "Really," she says, *sotto voce*.

Stumbling over one another, Cornwall and Albany leap off the deck to join Lear, cavorting around with him with mock salutes, shouting him down with nonsensical interruptions. Lear swings around on them angrily.

"It is not your turn, fuckwits!"

They are to follow in the procession of players and will be required to simply bow and smile. It is the moment for Cordelia to appear, dressed in her Ophelia white, her voice low and clear, calling, *"For thee; oppressed king, am I cast down."* She is waiting behind the wheelbox for her cue, running her long golden hair through her fingers, eyes fixed on the far shore.

Gloucester wanders towards her from the wrong play, something stirring in his memory. *How now, fair Ophelia.* Are those his lines? He sees a figure in white floating on top of the water, doing slow cartwheels, still garlanded with flowers - nettles, daisies, crow flowers and long purples that maids call dead men's fingers. He wants to weep, because it is his daughter there, in the water, even though he has already been killed by the crazed Hamlet.

"Do the dead weep?" he asks her.

Lear draws his sword on the unruly Dukes. He'll spill their guts, by Christ.

"Out of the way, dogs, swine, offal!" As he swings his sword it makes a thin, whistling sound.

"Let Cordelia emerge!"

"If they do, then it is at night," Gloucester is saying to Cordelia. "That's why nobody can sleep properly. I don't believe any of us have slept properly for years."

Two or three more people have joined the village idiot and the dogs to watch the players come ashore. Children with bland, oddly incurious expressions. They watch as Cornwall falls over in an effort to get away from Lear's sword.

"I surrender!" he calls, giggling. "You can take me."

Ah, here she comes, sad as a dream, brushing past Gloucester. Her entry never fails to bring a gasp. A ghost in the flesh, each who sees her knows and is momentarily lost in the tide of it, that her beauty is of an age long gone. Gloucester, for one, flounders in his memory in search of that pristine time.

Edmund bumps in front of her, leading his loathsome pet ape, Caliban. Caliban is very pleased to be let out of the stinking hold of the *Earl of Southampton*. There is a deep rumble from inside his chest as he hops off the barge, arms akimbo, runs in front of Lear and the Dukes, barking dog-like at the shackers; three women now, and an old man, who are staring with apathetic, uncomprehending eyes. He stops and urinates generously on Cornwall who rolls frantically away, screaming in falsetto.

Lear approaches the animal, sword still drawn. This time he will put paid to the beast. They could throw its carcass into the river. Divide the guts between them.

Ignoring his approach, the ape begins to masturbate.

There's Curan, keeping out of the way on the stern with Banquo's Children and her best friend, Extra, with whom she shares all the minor roles; the King of France; Duke of Burgundy; a Gentleman attendant on Cordelia (their favourite role); an Officer employed by Edmund (their least favourite role); a herald; Servants to Cornwall; an Old Man; Tenant to Gloucester; a doctor and Knights in Lear's train. The hardest workers in the cast.

Curan wants to hide herself; that's just the way I am. Behind the wheelhouse, below deck, behind her hand, behind Fleance and Little Extra; anywhere from the sharp eyes of Edmund and the pitch gypsy eyes of Regan. Curan is only thirteen (she thinks) and she knows these eyes have pricked her out. Edmund grins her his big Edmund grin as he vaults over the side of the *Earl of Southampton* to rescue his beloved ape. Curan puts her hand on Little Extra's shoulder, feeling the chubby child's flesh beneath. Extra is watching her with hard eyes.

Cordelia finally appears by Lear's side and makes a short speech. Her voice comes from somewhere beyond her, beyond the low, sluggish river, the dull light and the curtain of cloud; the voice of a child who is yet a woman:

"*We are not the first*
Who, with best meaning, have incur'd the worst.
For thee, oppressed king, am I cast down;
Myself could else out-frown false fortune's frown.
Shall we not see these daughters and these sisters?"

Lear allows his sword to fall from the neck of the antic ape. He drops to his knees, casting a quick look at Edmund who leads Caliban back to the barge, heading for Curan. Lear's voice is thick with emotion:

"*We two alone will sing like birds i' the cage*

When thou dost ask me blessing, I'll kneel down
And ask forgiveness: so we will live
And pray, and sing, and tell old tales, and laugh
At gilded butterflies ..."

The Fool makes his entrance, pointing at Lear and singing to the audience, juggling three balls while catching his hat as it falls off.

"*He that has a little tiny wit,*
With a hey, ho, the wind and the rain
Must make content with his fortunes fit,
Though the rain it raineth every day."

He dances a small jig, spins around three times, catches his hat in his teeth, bows to the audience and departs.

The presentation is over and Lear begins to harangue the audience, further grown by two men with set uncomfortable faces and filthy shapeless clothes. They stare at Lear blankly as he shouts.

"Ladies and gentlemen of Babylon." Gestures widely to the shackers.

"We are The Shakespeare Company and we have come to bring you, our illustrious audience," he bows to the tired heads, "the greatest play ever written. Notice I said *The* Shakespeare Company. I didn't say the London Shakespeare Company or the Stratford Shakespeare Company or the Peking Shakespeare Company or any other goddamn Shakespeare Company." He shakes his royal stick and bangs it on the rotting wood of the jetty. "I said *The* Shakespeare Company because we are in all probability," bows low again, sweeping his cape in front of him and letting his hair rake the wind without loss of crown, "in the most improbable of probable worlds, in other words this world we here inhabit, the last and only Shakespeare Company in the world; all the rest having gone down," he throws his arms towards the ground, "into the darkness." He brandishes his stick and his face goes red the way it does when he is banishing Cordelia, his one true daughter in the First Act.

"And we, the players of the Company, standing before you now, are by that same horrible logic, the last true Players, each dedicated to holding high the Cornucopia of Culture." He looks up towards the sky, face suffused with wonder. "Let the Cornucopia of Culture give forth its light, in this case, the words of a long dead bard who may still sing to us, even in ratshit little places like Babylon. And there are plenty of them.

"We will perform for you in your town hall, or weather permitting, on your village green, or any other suitable venue, this very evening (for what other evening is there?), the tragical history of King Lear, an old man more sinned against than sinning, some say, who falls into the clutches of Unspeakable Evil," his eyes dilate with horror, "And does himself go down into the Darkness.

"Come! Bring your friends, your children. For payment we seek only food, some donation, some valuable we can swap upriver. Some villages do us proud and slaughter a goat or a pig…"

His voice is growing hoarse and the shackers are beginning to lose interest and wander away. The village idiot gets up and imitates Caliban, making guttural sounds and hanging his arms down to his feet. Only a few children stay to watch the unloading of the barge. Neither the fine pewter crown nor the brooch that gleams in the depthless light can hold the others, who vanish back into their hovels. The children ignore Lear, their interest centred on Caliban.

Lear ponders the chance of getting a little red meat out of this herd, these debased vacant-eyed cattle that go on, in the face of all evidence, calling themselves human; turning their backs on others to shove at the trough, damn their eyes, damn their stiff departing backs, their hopeless undeserved ignorance.

Lear turns from the *Earl of Southampton* and looks up-river. A fine haze has descended, obscuring the distance; a light dew has formed on his beard. The water drifts quietly under the makeshift planks that hold him up. Time and place conjoin. He breathes, slowly and deliberately.

It is important to keep breathing. One after another, gulps of damp air. Breath control is essential to any player, as he's told the cast many times. Soon he will have to face Edmund, the Dukes, and his own anger. The presentation was completely ruined, he cannot just let it pass, not with someone like Edmund. You have to see with whom you're dealing.

His stick always lies handy.

In the meantime, however, he lets the blood run out of his face. Best not to soliloquise or otherwise implicate himself. There are a dozen towns after Babylon; Edmund can be handled the way all hoons can he handled. Best concentrate on the particular, the act of breathing, the rushing water, the bulk of the river rolling under mist. There are more Babylons; the river goes on forever, practically speaking.

The Fool sneaks up behind him and sings quietly in his ear, the voice of a demon familiar:

"*Fools had ne'er less grace in a year;*
For wise men are grown foppish
And know not how their wits to wear
Their manners are so apish."

Lear turns on him, prepared to strike, but the Fool has already danced out of reach. Damn his eyes! His wide, painted mouth, which never opens but to utter words from the play. But this blatant creature with his hanging mouth and ferret glances is the consummate clown, and one of the best actors among them; the only surviving member of the original cast. You could know the Fool for years at a stretch and never know him better. A song could be made of a paradox like that.

Now he stands in front of Lear, thumbing his nose at the royal anger. Taking hold of his clown's suit by imaginary garters, he stands tall and cavorts in front of an imaginary mirror, looking at his face from either side and simpering.

"*When I do stare,*" he says to Lear sternly, "*see how the subject quakes.*"

Edmund moves between Curan and Extra, pushing Banquo's Children to one side. Little Extra ducks out of the way of his hand and Fleance skips to where Edgar, Oswald and the Dukes are starting to unload the *Earl of Southampton*. Edmund bends over Curan.

"Here, I want to show you something."

I try to move out of his way. He is still leading the ape and the animal stench of it is overpowering. He takes hold of my arm at the sensitive spot where it joins the elbow.

"Something you'll be happy to see."

I go to push him away but he manoeuvres me behind the wheelhouse on the river side where Cordelia earlier waited, running her fingers through her long blonde hair, gazing towards the farther shore. I wish thoughts like that wouldn't interfere. And I wish I had long blonde hair like hers. I could play Cordelia and breathe like a flute those fateful and foreknowing lines - *My life will be too short and every measure fail me.*

Somewhat hidden from the others, Edmund undoes his shirt. Curan has seen this before. Everyone has. A sharp-eyed bird, an eagle perhaps (Curan has never seen an eagle), brightly tattooed on Edmund's broad, hairless chest. In blue and deep cochineal, it has been put on with the sure touch of an artist; so lifelike that when he flexes his muscles, causing them to ripple beneath the skin, the bird's tongue moves suggestively in and out, its eyes rise and fall, talons stretch and contract.

Curan swallows back bile. The stench of Caliban almost makes her faint. It's a thick coating on her throat. The animal is watching her with yellow, unwinking eyes, its hands lost in the fur between its legs. The hard planking of the wheelhouse digs into her shoulders. Edmund begins to croon.

"Oh you should be so lucky, Curan, my beauty, to be around when the eagle spreads her wings," he gently strokes the bird's head. "But look. You haven't seen all. The special effects. Notice the eye. Its wonderful sharp eye. Here is the mystery: what is it looking at? Can you guess, Curan? Can you see?" He grins his big Edmund grin at her.

Despite herself, Curan cannot resist a puzzle. Her eye involuntarily follows the line of the bird's sideways glance down to the plume of dark hair curling up to his navel, and down, as Edmund deftly unzips, to his already half-engorged cock; a heavy leviathan waking in his hand.

A sharp trick! Ha ha! A sharp trick indeed to catch an unwary courtier. He hefts it up and down in his palm, grinning with malice. The ape makes vaguely imitative gestures. A deep rumble comes from its chest.

Edmund is insane; that's why he's such a bad actor. He only plays himself but he's not as smart as the Edmund in the play. I push past him at last. Flashing his thing is about all he's good for, I tell him.

As she goes past, Curan's eye is caught by a movement on top of the wheelhouse. It is Kent, the dwarf, scuttling away before he is seen. As she looks up Edmund fingers her breast. Her skin withers. It doesn't show on him but he could be a carrier.

"Get away from me!" I tell him, loud enough for somebody nearby to hear.

Swinging his royal stick, Lear approaches Gloucester. Like his brooch and his pewter crown, the stick is one of his treasures, his rod of power. It is a straight piece of polished oak with a heavy brass knob. He taps his palm with the knob end as he squats down beside the Earl, who is sitting on the edge of the jetty massaging his arms.

"My arms are numb," he announces to Lear. "And here," he points to his fourth vertebra, "A horrible, pinching pain."

"Gloucester," Lear says, trying to keep his voice steady, "Can you tell me what the fuck is going on around here? Why Caliban was running around loose? Why Cornwall and Albany are pilled-out so early in the day?" He leans forward, his voice full of angry sibilants. "Jesus, Jesus, Jesus. Do I have to carry it all? The whole load? I put you in charge of the sub-plot, Gloucester. I give you a responsibility, like any good director. It's your reward for getting a major role. You have to kick a few arses. Like Edmund's, for example. You have full permission to cut the ape's throat at your discretion." He slams the brass end of the rod into his palm.

"We perform tonight, for Christ's sake, doesn't anyone understand that? We've got a performance to put in order."

Gloucester stares mournfully down at the water: then turns his stricken face to Lear.

"Truth is, Mainchance, I can't remember a single line. Not a word."

Lear buries his head in his hands. "Why do I bother, why do I bother?" a cracked and infinitely aged voice reiterates in his head. In the darkness behind his pressed palms he can see the stars and the wheeling galaxies. Are there other planets out there; planets still bathed in light? Wooded Hills? An ancient and eternal hope. Of course none of it is true. The other planets, the ones swinging behind his eyes, are nightmares of frozen methane gas or swirling heat or stark rock. Without life or sound, only the blowing death of rocks and gas and empty darkness. A vast continuum without voice, space or direction.

He opens his eyes on the real world in time to catch Gloucester bending over awkwardly to comfort him. He wants to put his arms around Gloucester's neck and pull him down and say to him, listen, Gloucester, I have had a terrible vision of empty illimitable spaces and the lifeless, inert worlds that inhabit them. Banishment. Banishment and damnation. We should kiss the ground we walk on, worship the least flower, nurture every young and quivering thing; forget the lavender water we were saving for our graves. We have all made a terrible, terrible mistake. I hear a voice which tells me of these things; it is cracked and infinitely aged.

Instead he allows Gloucester to put his hand on his royal shoulder. The faithful Earl has put on his white beard and his noble's costume, consisting of a dressing gown worn back to front and held together by rabbit skins slung around his waist as a belt.

"There, there, Mainchance," he says woodenly. "When have we ever let you down? We've been on the river too long, you and I. The show goes on. My lines will turn up." He sets his jaw. "I'll know my lines before the curtain goes up." His hand moves mechanically up and down on Lear's shoulder.

For days now, perhaps weeks, there is something Gloucester has been trying to remember. Sometimes he glimpses it in the dark, sliding water or hears it approach through the lines of the play. It fills him with a haunted sense of familiarity, a constant *déjà vu*.

"We need you, Mainchance. Without you there would be no show."

Lear hoists himself to his feet.

"Don't call me that." His stick swings out to take in the whole cast. "Listen, all of you. To your roles! I don't want to hear you call each other by any other names but your cast names. No pet names, nick-names, assumed names, passport names, real names, childhood or any other names you like to name. Only by entering deeply into your role can you hope to play it. Tonight we perform. We play Babylon. Each one of us will be on the line to *deliver.*" He pauses, bends down to Gloucester and hisses in his ear, "I was going to mention something, Gloucester, what was it?" He dithers, panicking. "What the fuck was it?"

"Rehearsal," Gloucester says tonelessly. "You were getting around to talking about rehearsal." The word tolls its familiar chimes in Gloucester's ear, releasing a line from the play, one of his own, the first to come back to him: *This great world shall wear out to nought. Dost thou know me?*

"*Dost thou know me?*" he asks Lear.

With the return of this line arrives a dull and familiar terror, a terror so familiar that he cannot for one moment doubt its authenticity.

"Rehearsal!" Lear shouts. "That's our first priority. To find our venue and get a rehearsal underway. It's our only chance to get it right. To take pride in our work." He bites his lips, looking around for Edmund. "There are some of us here that think this is a circus. They should go and find one." He looks bitterly at the Fool, "Places for juggling acts and animal parades. The play, the play's the thing. The play alone is our concern. By doing this we keep the play alive. Can you conceive of worlds in which there is no play?" He opens his arms out wide. Wide enough to take in the village, the river, *the Earl of Southampton*, the world and all its cast, even the bleak and frozen worlds he has seen in his vision, fleeing from the touch of mind; the universe of motion and silence.

"Circus? Circus?" Edmund is coming out from behind the wheelhouse with a smirk on his face, doing up his trousers and still leading Caliban. He bows to Cornwall and Albany, his smirk widening. Cornwall salutes.

"A circus," Edmund repeats. "Before you can have a circus, you must have a ringmaster. The master must be able to find his own ring. And to find his own ring he must first," he puts his finger into his cheek and makes a popping noise, the sound of a cork leaping from a bottle, "pull his finger out."

The Dukes fall on each other's necks laughing. Cornwall blurts out, "And to find his finger he must first find his ring, which brings us back to the first point."

"Aye and a hard and sticky point it is too," says Edmund, pushing his finger between his lips and opening his eyes wide.

"Edmund!" Lear's voice is like the roar of a bull across the jetty. "*Tremble thou wretch that has within thee undivulged crimes.* Edmund, bastard son of Gloucester."

"Here comes the master now, in search of his ring," Edmund confides to the Dukes. Then, pulling himself erect, "Remember, stay in your roles now. The play! The play!" He pretends to play a lute, jiggling his fingers against his crotch.

They are standing at the edge of the jetty, where the barge is moored. Lear arrives, swinging his royal stick.

"I see you are already too much in your role. Take care! I tell you, scum, you upstage anyone tonight with your stupid side-show tricks or bring that stinking animal anywhere near the stage and by Christ," he flips his stick into his left hand and draws his sword, which shines with a lethal brightness, no toy this, or papier-mâché prop, "I'll shove this through your gizzard!" The sword swoops through the dark air.

In mock surrender Edmund simpers in front of him while Cornwall and Albany giggle. Oswald joins the audience, standing a little to one side, a sardonic smile playing around his lips. Regan is also watching, from the deck, her eyes fastened onto Cordelia who has joined Lear. Now that a sufficient audience has gathered, Edmund begins to babble feverishly in an ecstasy of fawning obedience, rolling his eyes around in his head until nothing but whites show. "Yes m'Lord, no m'Lord. I'll catch you a pig for supper, m'Lord, juicy 'n tender 'n finger licken'." He curls his tongue around his finger deliciously, going cross-eyed for the benefit of the Dukes who are avidly awaiting his every move. He makes loud smacking sounds of satisfaction with his lips, "roasssst ssssuckling pig, m'Lord, three bags full, m'Lord, my Liege, my Lord; how does your garden grow, m'Lord? With little cockle shells?" He has not yet done up his shirt and is able to move his muscles as he talks so that the eagle winks at the Dukes who press their lips together and go red in the face. "And if we can't find a pig, m'Lord, you'd better eat goat; and if we can't find a goat, m'Lord, you'd better eat cow; and if we can't find a cow, m'Lord, you'd better eat dog; and if we can't find a dog, m'Lord, you'd better eat snake; and if we can't find a snake, m'Lord, you'd better eat shit; and if we can't find any shit, m'Lord, you'd better eat yourself," he leans forward and gazes with frank hatred into Lear's eyes, the playfulness gone from his voice, "For I tell you, you old degenerate, we'll eat you ere the night is done." The eagle's red tongue slides back and forth as if moving in and out of Edmund's flesh. Cornwall and Albany shriek and clutch each other around the waist. Goneril joins Regan on the deck.

"Really," she says in a harsh stage whisper.

Lear lowers the sword until it is level with the bird's eye, just over Edmund's heart. The tip of the sword is rock steady. The cracked and ancient voice inside him tells him to strike now, to warm the steel with Edmund's blood. Cordelia puts her arm around him and speaks with soft authority.

"Come king, actor, actor-king; save your rage and your tears until later, when the audience has gathered and the curtain's risen." Her blue eyes lock coldly with Edmund's. "The play, the play, remember good king? If you run him through the gizzard now we'll lack an Edmund to play later, destroy him within the right boundaries of the stage, the confines of the verse."

"That's right, Mainchance," Gloucester nods his head encouragingly. "After all, one monkey don't stop no show." As if at a pre-arranged signal the Dukes, their arms still around each other, begin to dance unsteadily, kicking their legs up in the air and singing in ragged chorus:

"One monkey don't stop no show

dum-de-dum-de-dum-dum

One monkey don't stop no show."

As they sing, Edmund kicks Caliban, trying to force the animal into a semblance of dancing, all the time keeping his eyes fixed on the sword.

"I can never get the bastard to dance," he says to Lear.

Lear's eyes glaze over. He sees row upon row of avid faces, lit by the soft lights of the Crystal Theatre, a brief flash of the spectrum as the lights from the chandeliers catch necklaces of pearl and diamond. He squares his shoulders, *every inch a king*, not letting the sword waver.

"You're not worth a can of shit, Edmund, Cordelia's right about that. You're not worth dumping over the side. In truth, I should run you through now, while I have the chance. Then dispatch that silly brute that follows you. But why spill the blood of carrion?" He raises his sword again. "I'll spill your innards all over your feet."

Cordelia steps between them, easing Lear's sword aside. Her complexion is utterly white, yet smooth and creamy, giving the impression of richness and depth. Her voice is soft and mild, nonetheless implacable; no-one could ever think of denying a voice like that. She addresses Edmund.

"Sir, don't provoke him further if you value your days. I believe you don't know Lear. I believe you can't see his very real greatness. He ranks alongside the greatest Shakespearean actors of all time. He's right up there with Betterton and Garrick, Kemble and Kean. We are a Company, Edmund, not a band of marauders plundering and pillaging our way upriver; you know there are plenty of those and you can join them any time. But while you are here in the Company, Lear is our kind. Our director. Our producer and our star. Without Lear there would be no Shakespeare Company. We ply an honourable trade."

Edmund ducks to and fro as if trying to escape from a hard leash. He doesn't like this. This gentle tongue lashing. It sears him like corrosive acid. Cornwall and Albany are no longer laughing. Caliban pulls roughly at Edmund's arm and Edmund has to turn and kick the beast which turns and snarls at him, pulling its lips back from its yellow teeth.

The Dukes gather each side of Edmund, gleefully anticipating his humiliation at the hands of the fair Cordelia, so gentle, *so young, my Lord, and true*. They stare at him from close range, their eyes gleaming with predatory interest, pinwheels of light appearing and disappearing in the depths of their pupils.

Lear still stands, sword raised, as if in tableau. Edmund cowers before Cordelia, who takes Lear's arm and turns to go.

"Beware, Edmund," she gestures to the ape, "You do not keep very intelligent company."

Once she has gone, leading Lear, Edmund seizes each Duke by the neck and holds them in a tight horse grip until their tongues loll out and their eyes rotate upward.

"I promise you one thing, my little sweeties, my little tasty morsels, my darling camp followers," shakes them a little, "I will have *her* down before me spread out like a plate of rabbit stew, hot stew done to a nice turn." He lets the dangling Dukes fall. "The eagle will fly then, my darlings, oh it will fly." Sensuously, he strokes the bird's wings stretching across his chest and nipples, grinning at Regan who is about to turn away.

"We'll pin her to the ground like a squealing sow," he calls to her, "So help me, as I am the Bastard Edmund and want no other name." He turns menacingly to the Dukes. "And you will help me, my lovies, won't you? You'll get your hands out of each other's pockets when the time comes, won't you? There'll be as tasty a pot as you've dipped your slidy fingers into in a long time."

The Dukes stare dumbly as he takes from his pocket a small flat tin. Immediately their eyes swivel towards it. Edmund shakes it gently back and forth. Pills slide from one end of their tin universe to the other. Cornwall and Albany nod their heads and giggle. Oh yes, yes Edmund, we'll have our hands out of our pockets. We'll have our wits in our hands. Anything. Anything.

The Dukes fall back and Edgar approaches. He is in time to see the small tin Edmund is putting back in his pocket.

"*Tom's a cold*," he says.

For Curan, emerging from the combined stench of Edmund and Caliban into the gypsy presence of Regan is like moving from a fetid swamp into a spring garden richly laid with flowers. The wild, dark-eyed, dark-haired sister takes her scent from a tiny prismatic bottle that she hides in the inner pocket of her jerkin, dabbing it scantily every morning with sharp pecking gestures. It is an airy, flowery scent, of summer and ocean winds. But beneath it there is a heavier, surer odour that belongs to the woman herself; a heady sweetness, an ambrosial intoxication. I can never stand near Regan and keep my breath steady. No-one understands her; she came to us from out of the mountains, her eyes dark and large as moons, a red scarf knotted in her hair. For weeks she followed us upriver, and like a wild animal she would come a little closer to our camp each evening. A little closer to the food and the warmth. Then she would join us to eat, only to vanish back into the night without uttering a sound once the food was gone. Finally she stayed with us and learned her part with alacrity, as if she knew the lines before they were read to her. Lear taught her her part patiently each night, training her for the role as she'd been trained to the campfire, Cordelia assisting, for she had never learned the skill of reading.

"Little Curan," she says condescendingly, placing her arm over mine as we stand at the top of the stairs leading down into the hold. "Are the jocks beginning to sniff around? That will happen. You can't hide the smell of blood. Not from jackals like that," she gestures in Edmund's direction.

Curan blushes. I hate blushing, especially around Regan. Of course there are few secrets on a barge, little room for privacy, but I can't stop the rush of blood to my head.

The warmth of her arm seeps into mine; is she going to notice me? The *little* Curan. Sweet little Curan only recently a woman. How much she has to learn, ho hum. My breasts are still small, no more than nascent swellings, while Regan's are full, woman's breasts, made even fuller by the shape of her 'Elizabethan' blouse with its puffed sleeves and frilly front cut low and oval.

Curan can feel the woman's eyes beating at her temple so she concentrates on the smooth decking of the barge. Step on a crack and you marry a rat. Sometimes you have to step on the cracks.

Curan is suddenly scared by this strange woman at her side who smells of exotic times and places; a woman whose mere presence becomes unbearable. Finally she is forced to take a deep breath and the plangent, milky odour that fills the air causes her to hallucinate.

A flower of peculiar construction. One long stem capped by a wheel made of intertwined fibres attached to the stem by fine green filaments. Hanging from the wheel are four crystals, red, green, blue and yellow in turn, each catching the light, gathering it, and tossing it out to her. When the mingled rays strike her eyes there is a sound as of bronze or gold and a thrill of pleasure passes through her body (step on a crack you marry a rat, step on a crack you marry a rat).

A light breeze strikes the flower and the wheel begins to rotate, pulling the crystals after it. The heavy crystals swing ponderously and collide in bursts of light that turn her skin transparent. Briefly she can see her own veins, muscles and internal organs; the flowing sheath of her skin. Beneath that, the water slipping by and the dark opacity of the earth. Her skeleton shows up, thin and bare wired, like the flower of some exotic plant. As the wind dies the crystals slow again, throwing their light in lazy arcs across her face, red, blue, green, yellow. Her skin thickens back over her bones.

She realizes that the unusual flower is as tall as she is. As soon as she has established this perspective, herself as a measure of something, the flower begins to diminish, to recede from her vision as if into the vacuum of space. Another appears, diminishing with it. More appear until there is a glittering field of them.

The background comes into focus. It is a small glade surrounded by broadleaf trees. Rolling in the grass, among the flowers, are two naked figures. She is watching from a distance, a part of the forest, the eyes of the forest. She can feel her body, distended and large, swinging beneath her. She leans forward to get a better look at the figures in the grass and bumps her head against Regan's arm.

Goneril is coming up the stairs from the living quarters below deck, moving carefully in keeping with her pregnant state. She waves away Regan's proffered arm and looks straight at Curan, who has suddenly developed a great interest in her own toes. Step on a crack you marry a rat.

"I see you have them swooning over you now, sister," Goneril says in a hollow, stentorian voice. Regan smiles at her prettily.

"Just because you've turned into a cow there's no need to start mooing, sister," Regan replies in a sweet voice. "Go tend your udders with your oils and leave swooning for those who are best able."

Goneril is tall and all angles, her face heavy jawed. She is carrying the farthingales, the understructure of hoops that will hold out her dress Elizabethan style and hopefully disguise her condition from the audience. She gives Regan a slow, half-lidded look, before turning back to Curan.

"Take my advice, young Courtier, despite our sister's poisoned silver tongue, stick with the women; at this court the men are all degenerates. Either that or they're fucked in the head. Or both. It's the old story with men; they have brought the darkness down upon us and I can't even promise my lamb, my poor dove," rubs her bulging womb, "the sight of the dear sun. This darkness is upon them and upon their eyes.

"Know that in women's company is the highest pleasure. Even men, blighted though they are, have some dim intimation of that. But at this court Shakespeare rules and Lear gets to call down the thunder, make an idiot of himself. I wouldn't judge all verse by this barbaric stuff. In Shakespeare women are all shrews or angelic sluts like our fair sister Cordelia, too good to be real. Have you heard of Sappho? Listen:

' ... how the air was rich in scent
of queenly spices made of myrrh
you rubbed smoothly on your limbs
and on soft beds, gently, our desire
for delicate girls
was satisfied.'"

She recites the lines with heavy emphasis on the accents, her voice booming over the barge and across the dilapidated jetty, at the same time raising her arms over her head in a childlike gesture, making a graceful dancer's arch.

"Would you like to hear more?" She fumbles around behind her among the farthingales and brings out her lute. She claims it is a genuine Elizabethan lute stolen by her from a museum. As she sings she strums several dulcet chords.

" ' ... let us sing to her

who wears the scent of violets
on her young breasts.'
Here's one for pleasant dreaming.
'Then I said to the elegant ladies
- how will you remember when you are old
the glorious things we did in our youth!
We did many pure, beautiful things.
Now that you're leaving the city,
Love's sharp pain encircles my heart.'"

She completes the last line with a few notes spaced for effect, staring mournfully into Curan's eyes.

Regan leans forward, "And what about that, sister darling?" running her hands smoothly over Goneril's belly. "How did the 'delicate girls' manage that? Perhaps they inflated you with their fragrant breaths. What is inside here, the scent of violets?"

Curan cannot watch Regan's fingers sliding over Goneril's belly. The hands are light and pale with flat dark hairs at the wrists. They are murderer's hands; I have seen them twist like a claw and leap for Gloucester's eyes. Such hands are barely tamed animals, sudden and unpredictable.

Goneril speaks ponderously, her voice almost as heavy and as deep as a man's. As she speaks she plucks the lute occasionally, punctuating her sentences with archaic notes.

"I'm worried about you Regan, I think you're seeing too much of Edmund; hardly the right influence, I'm sure you'll agree. As for my state, this is something I must do for the world if the world is to be ongoing. Every woman free of the Sickness, whatever her desires in the matter, should have a child by an uninfected man." She rests the lute against the wheelhouse and spreads her arms, much as Lear does in the storm scene.

"To bring one more pure being into the world, sisters, is our holy duty, otherwise how will womankind flourish?"

"And where," says Regan silkily, "are you going to find an uninfected man at this court?"

Disdaining to answer, Goneril turns back to me. She looks hard into my face.

"Growing pretty are you, sweetmeats?" caressing me under the chin. "Give me your hand, I want to show you something. Come, don't be shy. There'll be time later for swooning with Regan." Imperiously, "Your hand, sweetmeats. Never fear, I'm not going to tell your fortune. I'll leave that sort of thing to the witches. Only a fool would read her palm these days," glancing down at my hand, "And you, sweetmeats, are not even ripe enough for your lines to have firmed. It is given to some of us to have an open fate."

The skin of her fingers is oddly rough on the back of my hand; her thumb sits plumply on my palm.

"I wish to show you something of the estate into which you are coming," portentiously, "I mean the estate of womanhood. That holy estate men would violate with their monstrous organs. It is a cruel jest of nature that men are this way, yet inevitable, for they are as brief and as blind as their seed. Take my advice, use men only as you find them, not as they find you. They are, after all, poor dislocated creatures we women must harvest to pollinate ourselves. Feel this."

She places Curan's hand on her breast. It is heavy and strangely lumpy beneath my fingers; the impression of clotted veins and knotted tendons. "Gentle, sweetmeats, gentle; that's milk inside there. The milk of life. It is the same milk that flows through the breast of every woman. If you sucked now there would be a thin, sweet trickle. If you're curious, try it. Every woman who has lived, is living, or will ever live, has bathed in this milk; it is formed out of our very blood and it teaches us to nurture. Try it, try it. Think of it as a river whose origins are lost in time and which flows through our flesh and out into the world.

"That is what the men have never learned, sweetmeats; to nurture and to nourish. No milk flows through their vestigial tits. They are a blind rush and an anonymous death. In that they learn only to corrupt and destroy, bringing upon them the doom of heaven. These are historical facts."

I glance across at Regan. She is watching Goneril's performance with a thin smile. Goneril has more or less forgotten both of us, although she still holds my hand to her breast.

"When the milk begins to flow we understand something. Have you wondered, child, what you are, what the estate of womanhood is? Let me tell you. We are of one flesh; we are one many-breasted creature. Go on, try it," she pulls me closer. "It is the taste of your childhood and your death; your changeling immortality. Try it! Know the taste of your own body."

Lear pushes past the women clustered at the top of the stairs, catching a brief glimpse of Curan's discomforted face, and retreats down into the cramped gloom of the barge's living quarters. Here in serried bunks and pillowed corners most of the cast sleep and live out their river existence. The candle still burns on the small table supporting the mirror where Lear earlier preened himself.

He doesn't stop to glance at it now but heads directly to the ornate trunk that sits in the corner where he and Cordelia sleep. Throwing off the clothes that are heaped on it, he opens it and digs down past the copies of Shakespeare, the Collected Plays and smaller performance editions, to pull out the large black book he keeps wrapped in silk. Feeling the loneliness, the coldness of the stark reaches of space, he is always drawn back to it and the words of the voice that claimed to be the Lord of those other reaches, and Lord of princes too. There were many clues given as to how such a Lord would destroy the world.

Carefully he unfolds the silk, patterned in carnations and roses, and takes the book in his hand. He knows the passages his eyes will seek, and sure enough they seek them out like the fruits of forbidden knowledge. Mouthing the words as they rise up to him, he reads them haltingly, like a child.

And the second angel followed, saying, fallen, fallen is Babylon the great, which hath made all the nations to drink the wine of the wrath of her fornication... And he carried me away in the Spirit into the wilderness: I saw a woman sitting on a scarlet-coloured beast, full of names of blasphemy, having seven heads and ten horns. And the woman was arrayed in purple and scarlet, and decked herself with gold and precious stones and pearls, having in her hands a golden cup full of abominations, even the unclean things of her fornication. And upon her forehead a name was written. MYSTERY, BABYLON THE GREAT, THE MOTHER OF HARLOTS AND THE ABOMINATIONS OF THE EARTH.'

Lear sits down on top of the trunk, squinting at the words in the dim light.

And he cried with a mighty voice saying, fallen, fallen is Babylon the great, and has become the habitation of devils, and a hold of every unclean spirit, and a hold of every hateful and unclean bird.'

With a decisive motion, Lear slams the book shut and wraps it back in its gaily coloured silk. Here is the key to his agony, in these wild words. A violent deity has withdrawn his grace from the world. Now bits of it are falling away, great chunks of it falling like banks of a river under flood, falling into the greyness and darkness.

Lear knows the process of the Lord's withdrawal from the world.

First the colours go, the greens, the yellows, the blues, all the colours of celebration; a greyness lies over everything, the greyness of heavy cloud, the peeling grey of the Sickness, the corruption of curs, whelps and fatlings, food for kites and buzzards. Then the shapes go, the sharp even lines of the horizon, the intricate stitching of the stars, the gracious outline of a coast; all lost to a dull haze that sets the teeth of form on edge and obliterates beauty.

This is the way the world is lost. Bit by bit. Piece by piece. A little here, a little there. Chunk by chunk. Separated and pulverized to a fine dust good only for scouring the bones. Moment torn from moment. Gesture from gesture. Word from word. Until there is nothing but the echo of absence, poor Gloucester, and a crusty huddle of shacks where once a great city thrived.

It is all there, in the black book, which weighs in his hand, thick and ineluctably heavy. He hears a rustling, as of huge wings passing in some alternative space. He's felt something similar, looking into Cordelia's eyes as she lies close to him. Her eyes shine as if he is looking into something empty, containing vast stretches of space; a universe in her skull yet so far away he cannot enter it. It is at such moments he feels close to deciphering his existence.

The rustle comes again, but this time more distinctly. Lear turns. It is not an angel of wrath or a bird in some alternative space but Kent, the dwarf. Kent bows low.

"I'm sorry to interrupt your meditations, Lord," he says in a thin, ingratiating voice, "But it is important. It's a matter of my costume. Well, not really the costume but the role. I'm supposed to be banished in Act I Scene I and return in disguise in Scene IV, but I don't have a costume for my return. All I have to indicate to the audience that I'm in disguise, is this." He holds up a towel which has, admittedly, seen better days, patterned with the card pack. He holds it as one might a dead rodent by the rail.

"The Fool would be better off with this," Kent says.

Mention of the Fool brings Lear back to the present moment. There is work to be done.

"Talk to Cordelia," Lear says brusquely. "She's in charge of costume. There must be something else in the rag box." He pushes past Kent and makes for the stairs.

Kent follows him up onto the deck. What can he do with a towel but wrap it around his head like a scarf? Then he looks like a little old woman. That makes him look ridiculous and the audience starts throwing things. It is ridiculous. It strips his role of all dignity.

"Is that what you want?" he asks Lear insistently.

On deck the unloading has begun. Lear collects Oswald, Cordelia and Gloucester and heads into the village to seek a stage. Kent follows along, still talking, appealing now and then to Cordelia or Oswald. Kent has the body of a child, with a child's tiny hands and feet, yet his head is the head of a man; too big for his body, with a large bulging brow and wide, thick lips.

"No-one listens to a dwarf," he complains to Oswald, "You have to be at least five feet tall to be taken seriously." His voice is that of an adult, yet without timbre, thin and piercing.

Oswald walks along in silence, appearing not to hear. He walks a little apart from the others; the only member of the cast to show the familiar blotchy signs of the Sickness. He feels it as a creeping lethargy, a slow pumping out of the life that is inside him, as if the raw force of entropy itself has taken root in his blood. A coldness working outwards from the bone.

At the same time he knows a queasy pleasure, the satisfaction of the doomed, the release from anxiety; knowledge that the sentence is passed and the execution well along the way. How the heathlings live in fear of waking up one morning and finding their skins so marked. It is amusing to watch them strut and shout and rage at the gods.

His own role he treats with contempt - Oswald is a worm hardly worth stepping on, audience and players alike agree. In learned works, his part in the unfolding of events is passed over in virtual silence. He is despised by all; and most particularly by those who use him for advantage. All and all it is a role that outfits him well for the Sickness, and for which the Sickness well outfits him; a role he suffers like the Sickness, with detachment and secret glee.

He knows a few things, however, does Oswald, Steward to Goneril, things he would never tell except perhaps to the Fool. Separated from humanity by the taste of death, he has become its most cynical observer. He can watch others. Divine their secrets just by watching, reading their smallest movements. Be a double agent for death. The fast approaching final weariness as the spirit drains from the body has sharpened his eyes no end to the vulnerabilities of the flesh. What he has seen and understood has made him empty, and that is how he walks along, listening to the conversation but not part of it, camping in the flesh but not rooted there, taking in the air and expelling it without hope or dream.

You can't say that Oswald, Steward to Goneril, is walking towards the grave with his eyes closed.

Meanwhile Kent has returned to pestering Lear, running to keep up, pulling at Lear's sleeve and whining about his role.

It is not plausible, he complains, to have him come back in disguise in Act I Scene IV, towel or no towel. The towel really has nothing to do with it. How can a dwarf return in disguise anyway? It makes Lear look like a fool for not recognising him instantly, and Lear's wits are not yet supposed to have turned. How he hates the audience snickering when he has to say *I do profess to be no less than I seem*. It makes nonsense of Kent's role as defender of Lear. It would be better to have him in some other role. There are problems with Gloucester too at the end of Act II Scene II, where Kent is in the stocks. All the other players exeunt and Gloucester is left to commiserate with Kent who, in turn, gets the opportunity to make a reflective speech before Scene III. The problem is,

41

Gloucester always forgets to stay on stage and they have to skip Kent's speech. Because of this Kent never gets the chance to deliver his favourite lines, *Fortune, good night, smile, once more turn thy wheel.*

As he talks he casts sidelong glances at Gloucester, pitching his voice so that Gloucester cannot help but hear.

Is it in any way fair, Kent enquires of anyone who might be listening, to have his scene cut short this way? Gloucester claims he simply forgets, but Kent is not fooled. Not on your nelly. How come he never 'forgets' to *leave* the stage with the others? He does often enough in other scenes. It's well known that quite often players coming in for the next scene have to shunt Gloucester off stage first.

And another thing, what about Kent drawing his sword on Oswald, apparently intimidating him? How can any audience buy that? He'd be better off in some other role. Is it plausible to have a dwarf fight Edmund and apparently fatally wound him? No wonder audiences throw things at him. Even Oswald's part would be preferable. Or Gloucester. Now there's a role for an actor! Kent already knows Gloucester's part better than Gloucester does. What sweet pathos a dwarf could bring to Gloucester's part. Here he is defying Regan and Cornwall. Listen:

"*I would not see thy cruel nails*
Pluck out his old eyes, nor thy fierce sister
In his anointed flesh stick boarish fangs.
The sea, with such a storm as, in hell black,
no, wait, it goes,
The sea, with such storms as his bare head
In hell black night endured, would have buoy'd up
And quench'd the stelled fires ... "

"Enough, enough!" Lear knows the speech; he knows the whole play word for word, a hastily conceived creature of the mind, no need to quote it at him. Kent should be satisfied with what he is. It is a noble role. In a play full of villains Kent's integrity and faithfulness become important moral principles. Kent stands early with Cordelia for honesty and forthrightness. Without them the play would lose all dramatic balance, tipping over on itself into horror and degradation, insanity and cruelty, not tragedy at all.

Lear nods to himself, pleased with his ideas. Dramatic balance. It is the key to the successful staging of the play. Perhaps the part of Kent *is* too important for the snivelling dwarf.

A few faces peer from wretched doorways as they pass. Frightened, uncomprehending faces. And something else Lear finds hard to pin down, something frightening that cannot be identified with any particular quality. On the face of it Babylon is just like a hundred other places. The shacks are thrown together out of junk materials; drums, tins, bits of packing cases, sections of cars, crates, pallets and random lumps of wood.

There is no need for people to live like that; every city and town is more than half deserted and in some cases completely abandoned. Mansions stand empty and serve as homes to goats and chickens. Whole extant villages are overgrown. People come to places like this fleeing the Sickness, bringing it with them, spreading it further as they run from it; ending up in charnel houses like Babylon with nowhere left to go. Not the time to find a quiet place to die.

The darkness is too thick for the light of culture, the grandeur of tragedy. There is nothing here, no possibility but the commonplace stench of death. Of course Lear has seen such villages before. The stench of death and moaning of the dying are nothing new to him, nor the perpetual half-light emitted by the low cloud.

A group of shackers stand at the end of the street, watching the small party of players approach. As they draw near, Lear can feel the pressure of their blank, indifferent stares. These are people already dead, he thinks, but have failed to leave their bodies. Corpses, forced into the simulation of life by spirits too terrified to enter the afterworld.

Gloucester too is affected.

"You'd think they'd never seen human beings before," he remarks to Lear. "They'll wear out their eyes with staring."

"To a town this size the river is an ocean," Lear replies.

"Perhaps they think we are gods," Gloucester says.

After they have passed the group of shackers, Lear cannot help but turn around and glance back, hardly believing that they would still be there, that they did not vanish as soon as the players passed them.

Cordelia takes his arm and smiles at him.

They find their stage at the end of the street where a deserted church marks the boundary between the ragged dwellings and the spiny forest. Lear notices that the ground to one side of the church slopes down into a natural amphitheatre. There is a graveyard behind the church upon which the forest is encroaching.

Entering the old graveyard and examining the forest closer, Lear notices that the trees also have their sickness to deal with; it is the bitter rain that falls from the North. Many of the trees are a stunted, twisted parody of their genetic forms. In some cases their efforts to grow branches have resulted in twisted humps in the trunk, open and running with dark sap. A whitish mould grows over the gravestones, turning them lumpy and misshapen. The graveyard does not so much seem empty as vacated, as if the spirits themselves have long since moved on.

"We've played worse places than Babylon," he tells the others when he appears from behind the church.

The rest of the cast have already started arriving, Cordelia and Curan are marking out the stage. Ropes will be erected to delineate the seating areas. The huge dark curtains that make up the stage walls will be slung between sturdy tent poles. Their pride and joy, the large stage lanterns, will be lit and hung.

A ripple of pre-performance excitement passes through them all.

Lear beats the ground with his royal stick, shouting orders and sweeping a low bow to the gathered throng of stately Babylon. A rosy tinge touches Cordelia's cheeks. Curan and Extra giggle and hold hands. Edmund, Edgar and the Dukes arrive with most of the props. Edmund lets Little Extra stroke the eagle's head. Fleance shows Edgar how he can do somersaults.

Gloucester walks with heavy steps, his mouth moving as he searches out his speeches. They are coming back to him now, bit by bit, piece by piece; parts of the play reassembled, set in motion. Motion of which he too is a part and of which he is only partly aware.

He knows he is no more than a sleepwalker in these events; his acting is atrocious, he'd be the first to admit. The best he can hope to do is position himself on stage as correctly as possible and repeat the lines word by word. He will do that for Mainchance's sake, hardly understanding a word he is saying, nor three-quarters of the play for that matter.

Although the play is returning to him now, in the long term, over a series of weeks, days, it is slipping away from him. Sliding as a dream does, down to the muddy bottom. His real life is lived elsewhere, in some place he cannot quite recall. As the play returns, as it slips away, words detach themselves and float free of their context. They come to him from a far distance; half remembered meanings come and go, haunting the lines. People in wild costumes come up to him and thrust their faces into his, shouting things at him, connive against him, abuse him; and he hears his own voice answer mechanically, unwinding the lines like a piece of clockwork - at least, at the best of times.

There (enough of the play has returned for it to have slipped into view) in the half-meanings and the shadows, the metronomic voice of the play, the flattened horizon of gesture and ratiocination, is the terror; the blind terror that shuffles towards him, arms outstretched, intoning: *All dark and comfortless.*

Curan stays close to Cordelia as the preparations go forward. Cordelia is the centre of a circle of protection that ensures Curan's immunity from the prying eyes of Edmund and the gypsy presence of Regan. While

Regan fascinates the young courtier, it is Cordelia she admires and longs to be like. *So young, my Lord, and true.* Cordelia supervises the setting up of the stage, and both Curan and Extra jump to her gentle commands.

The stage will resemble a room with one wall removed and the two side walls opened out at an angle. The props consist of simple cardboard pillars of vaguely classical line for the inside scenes, Lear's Palace and Gloucester's Castle; while a couple of branches from the surrounding forest will be used to suggest the heath.

Cordelia organises it all with an authoritative calm; out of heaped boxes of clothing a wardrobe and make-up space appear, two tents arise; out of lumps of timber and cloth the stage takes form; the lanterns are carefully hefted into place; Edgar is dispatched to the forest for some branches. Order and purpose spring into being and things gravitate as if by magnetic force to their rightful place.

As I work I murmur Cordelia's lines and she corrects me. I know that she has chosen me for her understudy although nothing's been said. I know all her lines already, and it's just a matter of getting the intonation right. *Time shall unfold what plighted cunning hides; who covers faults at last shame them derides.* Sensing the slope and shape of the words, pitch and timbre, running them around my tongue until they become natural and inborn. *If for I want that glib and oily art/ To speak and purpose not.*

I take precedence over Extra, who's younger and envious of my favour with Cordelia. I am always reassuring my friend that I have no designs of Cordelia's role. I praise Cordelia to the skies, exclaiming on what a perfect Cordelia she is. No-one could play the role as she does; create out of this mess a production, a play, but the fair Cordelia. Who else?

"The truth is," I confide to Extra, "I am in love with Cordelia."

Edgar grinds his teeth until his head hurts. He must stop grinding them or he'll end up like some toothless old dog by the side of the road. It is a reflex of the jaw, probably some side-effect from Edmund's pills. But why care about his molars? Long before they'll be any problem his deep-dark secret will have pulled him into the earth or buried him beneath the glassy surface of the river.

He is being sent into the forest by Cordelia. Is it a sign? In the moment she looked at him he fancied he saw the angel of death grinning at him. Should he slip away into the twisted, half-formed gloom, seek out some sheltered place and die?

Who is Edgar?

What is Edgar to him or he to Edgar? Often he's seen the sardonic smile that plays over the lips of Oswald the despised. Now he understands; now he can see things from Oswald's point of view. Edgar is a disguise, nothing more. A series of disguises, in fact. He can slide out from under the bustle of preparations and vanish. No-one will notice he is gone. No-one will look up and say "Where's Edgar?" At least not until rehearsal. It isn't a matter of self-pity. He can leave that sort of thing to Kent. It is simply a fact. No-one notices Edgar, least of all the pretty Curan.

Nor would he last long in the wilderness, if he chooses to wander. There are rumours of grotesque half-creatures, para-beings, who have developed a taste for human flesh by feeding on the corpses of Sickness victims. They are able, for a time, to assume human shape, that of an enticingly beautiful man or woman, and so lure their victims into a trap and a sweet death.

A brief, haunting vision of Curan comes into his mind. Not the Curan he has just seen who clusters adoringly around Cordelia, simpering and fawning with the other sycophants, blushing and giggling, but a mysteriously transformed Curan, ethereally beautiful: Curan as a para-being might copy her from the lineaments of his desire.

What kind of death would that be? Full of agony and pleasure? Easier to slide over the edge of the barge one night and let the greasy water cover him, drag him down. Burying him with his deep-dark secret. No more Edgar. No more disguises. No more river. No more visions of Curan with her pixie face and pixie breasts. No more deep-dark secret. No more star blasting and taking.

Tomorrow, tomorrow. It is best to hide inside himself until tomorrow. It will not be hard. He can put on his disguise. *Tom's a cold.* Make himself invisible until after the evening's performance.

As he approaches the forest he sees Edmund and the Dukes slipping into the trees. Hardly likely that they are on legitimate business. Lazy bastards. Perhaps Edmund will get out his little tin again. In the pills there is forgetfulness and exhilaration, but there is no hiding his secret forever; the white patches on his buttocks tell their own story, and when they have migrated to his face he will become an outcast, a pariah, joining the despised Oswald to walk apart in isolation. To be avoided like a dog with the mange.

No thanks. Never. Put it up your bum. Rather the oily taste of death, the flaccid water closing around him; visions of Curan slipping away through the darkness. Curan he can never have, never kiss, never even touch. Certainly never declare his love. He can never intervene in her life. She might simper and fawn forever on the green of Babylon, making a fool of herself for that stuck-up bitch, Cordelia, that angel in the flesh - *So young; my Lord, and true.* La, la, la.

Still approaching the forest, he is noticed by Gloucester, who is sitting off to one side, murmuring to himself. Gloucester gets up and approaches him, gripping his arms fiercely.

Gloucester: "*Dost thou know the way to Dover?*"
Edgar: "*Aye, master.*"
Gloucester: "*There's a cliff whose high and bending head*
Looks fearfully in the confined deep;
Bring me but to the very brim of it,

And I'll repair... I'll repair... I'll repair..." He breaks off, mumbling.

"*... the misery thou dost bear,*" supplies Edgar.

"*... the misery thou dost bear,*" repeats Gloucester.

"*With something rich about me,*" supplies Edgar, getting tired of the game.

"*With something rich about me,*" repeats Gloucester, for whom the play is beginning to distend at each end into an impossible length. The first scene bends off into the beginning of the world, his last lines, in full, are still lost in the mists of the future.

Gloucester is stranded in the blind middle, glimpsing only a bitter moor. *No further, sir, a man may rot even here.* That one line, his last, has detached itself and floats back to him from the future. He is reasonably sure it is his last line. Nothing seems to come after. Act V Scene II; farewell to Gloucester, and for Edgar yet another hasty disguise.

How can Gloucester possibly remember all the lines, from now until then? This unnatural distending of the speeches is a new and frightening symptom, and his neck and shoulders ache from accumulated tension. They have been aching all along, he realizes. Nobody sleeps properly. He looks helplessly at Edgar who is looking bored and impatient, glancing towards the forest.

"*With something rich about me,*" he repeats to Gloucester. Gloucester considers the words. Surely there is something about that fellow's voice? Of course. His legitimate son, Edgar, *the food of thy abused father's wrath.* Now the lines come to him.

"*... the misery thou dost bear,
With something rich about me
And from that place
I shall no leading need,*" he completes triumphantly, the fates of the play once again set ticking inside him. Blessed Edgar! He stalks the terror around the circle of the play, for it is there in lines that have not yet come to him. He sees the fingers of a woman, long and delicate, hook

themselves into the shape of a claw. A bird's claw. The memory seems to come from both the past and the future; it flees into the future and plods after him from behind. As long as he remains here, with his legitimate son Edgar, he is safe.

Edgar levers the Earl's fingers from his arm, his eyes still seeking after Edmund and the Dukes. How difficult it is to shake loose from the old fart.

"Piss off, you smelly old goat!" Edgar hisses in his ear. "Do you piss in your pants now? Have you grown incontinent? Are you incapable of looking after yourself? You look drunk to me. Be on your way!"

Gloucester holds on with grim strength. "*I have no way and therefore want no eyes,*" he mouths. His eyes are tightly shut.

"Open your eyes!" Edgar shouts. "You've no more brain than Edmund's ape. Open your eyes!"

"*Ah! Dear son Edgar,*
The food of thy abused father's wrath;
Might I but live to see thee in my touch
I'd say I had eyes again."

Edgar shakes free, having to twist the old man's wrists to do so. "Find your eyes, old man. Go find Lear or Cordelia. Or someone who can deal with you." He twists his mouth up. "*Tom's a cold. Poor Tom hath been scared out of his wits,* and so lacks the wit to house his brain and wraps his secret to himself where it may fester even into madness; all the while his brain floats down the river, old man, a soggy, maggoty thing like your own. Ha ha! Food for fish and eels. Go find your eyes but have no fear; tomorrow there will be no more Edgar except some dreadful thing should take his shape and mimic out his lines." He makes a grotesque face and imitates himself on stage, exaggerating his gestures, crooning, "*As I stood here below methought his eyes were two full moons.* But tomorrow, no more Edgar. No more poor Tom with his parrot cry, *Tom's a cold.* No more wild whirling words. The universe has grown ancient, old man, even within the space of a second. The earth dribbles spittle, the way you do. The stars have grown cold and icy. *Tom's a cold!* There's no comfort left in the mind of man but the suffocating dreams of water."

Gloucester hugs Edgar to him, tears streaming down his face. "I have memories," he babbles. "Memories that come from the future. From all around. I have been through this before. Perhaps many times. Everywhere I go I'm following my footsteps and I hear somebody walking behind. It is the same when I close my eyes." His eyes are again tightly closed. A voice whispers in his ear,

"*Our flesh and blood, my Lord, is grown so vile, that it doth hate what gets it.*"

As these new lines are taken and fitted into place, the mechanism of the play begins to clarify in Gloucester's mind. He nods his head wisely.

"It's a closed circle," he affirms, the terror stalking him close now.

The word 'rehearsal' tolls across the field. Gloucester opens his eyes to find that he is not hugging Edgar, as he believed, but the trunk of a tree. Turning, he sees Lear gesticulating in the drizzly light. He is looking across at Gloucester and his arm is upraised, beckoning. He begins to walk towards the stage with slow, steady steps, the stage a stable referent in his field. After three steps the stage does not look appreciably larger, but the lay of the land is deceptive. Another step and he encounters Kent, who stands directly in front of him and twists him a stare of intense hatred.

"Gloucester, I want to talk to you. I think you know what about. It's the stocks scene, Act II, Scene II."

Gloucester ponders, opening a corridor through the lines and around the circle, past familiar landmarks in the action, entries and exits, betrayals and murders, grey blank patches yet to be filled in, to arrive at a picture of the dwarf, Kent in fact, locked in a wooden frame just to his size, members of the audience pelting him with rotten fruit and shouting insults.

Not a pretty part to play but there it is; he gets his moment of glory at the end of the play when he is able to throw off his peasant disguise and put forward his sword in defence of the King. Noble Kent! It is an ignominious scene to be sure, he tells Kent compassionately, every actor has such scenes he approaches with dread and terror. The play contains ignominious moments for all, everybody's nose gets rubbed in it; that is simply the nature of the play. Surely Kent can see that?

Apparently not. Which is a great pity. The smooth running of the sub-plot has been entrusted to Gloucester and this scene, he explains to Kent, the scene in question, generally falls within his jurisdiction, given a quibble or two on the boundaries of the sub-plot and the distribution of characters and scenes. Beside the fact that this is an ideal opportunity to show Mainchance that he can assume his full obligations and responsibilities to text, player and performance, you would think that an actor like Kent with a key role would appreciate the experience and guidance of an older player. And a little respect for authority, when that authority did in fact speak from experience and a thorough understanding of the dramatic principles involved.

In short, he must speak plainly with Kent, who will have to put up with his role just as Gloucester puts up with his. This is not *Love's Labour's Lost*. Does Kent think it is all violets and roses being Gloucester, being subjected night after night to the grossest humiliations, he pauses to tick them off: betrayed by the son he trusts; having his beard plucked and his hands tied. He stops in mid sentence. It is upon him now. He can see a woman's hand shaped into a claw. He knows that hand. He has always known it.

"Kent..." He trails off. He knows why the figure intones, *All dark and comfortless*. Why *all dark*? Wherefore *comfortless*? He has the answers. His body begins to shake, the muscles across the top of his spinal column ache chronically.

"Gloucester," says Kent in a cold, thin voice, "Do you remember lines, certain lines that begin, *I am sorry for thee friend; 'tis the Duke's displeasure, whose disposition all the world well knows, will not be rubbed or stopped?"*

The Earl simply stares down at Kent, remembering the lines and fitting them into place even as Kent speaks them. The play passes through his mind like a pack of cards being flipped, no single image holding long enough to be recognized. His heart is dilating and contracting painfully in his chest.

Kent steps forward and grabs the hem of Gloucester's dressing-gown threateningly.

"And you remember the lines," the thin insistent voice continues, "*I have watched and travelled hard; some of the time I shall sleep out, the rest I'll whistle?*"

Gloucester tries to step back but Kent is still clinging to his legs.

"Those are my lines," Gloucester says loftily, adjusting the rabbit skins around his waist and straightening his dressing-gown. "At this stage, Kent, we have to concentrate on our own lines, getting our own parts correct. I don't think…"

"Shut up!" Kent's voice breaks into a hoarse scream. "Shut up, shut up, shut up, you fucking gasbag." Kent leaps up and down, his face working with fury, his child's fists bunched.

"I'll kill you, I swear it. I'll find a way. I'll kill you. Don't you understand? After these lines I've got a speech that begins,
  … *Good King, that must approve the common saw*
  Thou out of heaven's benediction comest
  To the warm globe, I mean, *the warm sun,*
  the other bit goes,
  Approach thou beacon under this globe."

While he speaks Gloucester looks pityingly down at the raging figure. The pressure of Kent's role is obviously getting the better of him.

"… and I never get to deliver those lines that are my favourites. I never get to deliver them. They finish, *Take vantage, weary eyes,* no, that's the previous line.

Take vantage heavy eyes, not to behold
... This shameful lodging
Fortune, good night, smile once more; turn thy wheel."

"Don't worry about it," Gloucester advises Kent generously. "All the Kents you can imagine, no matter how good, and you must be one of the best, the best the Company has ever had, forget the odd line here and there." Gloucester gives a self-deprecatory laugh. Why, even an old hand like Gloucester himself might slip a cog here and there, drop a line, miss a cue. Such things are part and parcel of the business of acting. Along with rotten fruit and insults.

"Besides," he adds benevolently, "Being in the stocks is enough to make anyone forget a few lines. For myself, I'm only too pleased to get off the stage at the end of that scene." He adds, "Not all the rotten fruit finds its target."

As Edgar enters the forest he feels a subtle change of substance. In passing over he has become, to some limited extent at least, a creature of the forest. Looking back, the old church and the makeshift stage look smaller, flatter, leached of colour; the bush surprisingly thick and rich. The leaves whisper to each other, although the air is heavy and still. As he listens he seems to grow larger, expanding to fill the silence. He becomes aware of another sound. A harsh crackling noise like two rocks being rubbed together. It takes him a moment to recognise the sound of his own grinding teeth. He thinks, I wonder if the para-beings can hear me. Hear me think. The creatures that take human shape and prefer warm, living flesh to corpses.

He shivers.

If Curan were to appear to him now, dripping sweetness from her mouth, would he resist? There, among the trees, it is no longer an impossible fantasy that such creatures might live, mysteriously partaking in the life of the forest, living out their wretched half-lives among the twisted boughs. He has always taken it as a folk tale, a ghost story, but here in the forest with its shadows falling across his shoulders and the human world receding, it occurs to him that the forest and its creatures are part of a reality lying alongside, but not exactly continuous with, his human reality. Another dimension that interpenetrates the universe he walks and breathes in.

Certainly the trees and other plants are visible to the human eye, but perhaps they are mere surface configurations, a small part of a much larger whole. A much larger whole that doesn't want to be seen. Meeting something apparently familiar, like a forest, the eye digs no further. Perfect camouflage for a hostile and predatory species.

The lapping of another universe, he thinks, and the flesh hungry creatures that swarm out of it. Let Curan once appear and Edgar will, like Gloucester, walk over the cliff of his blindness. Something like that.

How would such a creature locate and track its prey? The best solution would be for it to tune in to human thought the way regular predatory beasts pick up olfactory signals. A smell can be disguised, changed, or even eliminated altogether, but who can stop a human being from thinking, and still keep them functional? Or disguise the process of human thought? Our compulsive broadcasting might make us beacons; creatures might be able to home in, even from the other end of the universe. From some end of another universe.

Thinking hard he broadcast the following message to any wraith creatures who might be listening:

"Better to embrace a false Curan, a simulacrum, to fall for a substitute creation, and so be devoured, than embrace the real Curan and infect her with my Sickness, pour poison into her body even with my love. To that extent she and I belong to different universes, and mine is fatal to hers. *Tom's a cold. Tom will throw his head at them. Avaunt, you curs!*

"This is why I am here," he continues beaming to the para-beings. "Not to follow Edmund or hunger after his pills or even to escape from the dreary Gloucester, still less collect branches for our mock heath, but to seek out just such a creature as yourself, as I imagine you to be with your terrible feral hunger. Why wait until tomorrow? The performance? The river? Surely, you brute listeners, this is my only and best and most noble course of action; and it is because I have no attachment to my role that I can see this. Edgar means nothing to me. His loyalties and concerns pale into insignificance. *Tom's a cold.* If I go on living it is to go on courting the doom of the flesh, for who can let go their love?

"Do you understand, you powers? I will not touch the rose I love to see it wither on the stem from that same touch."

Feeling very pleased with his speech, he eases forward, allowing the forest to enclose him, the shadows to lick him with cool, dark tongues. What do you do if food hops onto your tongue?

He hears Edmund's voice from ahead, low but distinct.

"Her leg, her leg, you pigswill, hold it down!"

The first thing Edgar sees is Edmund's ape, looking very much at home in the setting, its rheumy eyes emerging from a frame of green. Near it lies Edmund, spread-eagled on the ground with a Duke holding on to each leg.

"Further apart, further apart," he berates them. "A bloody baby could free itself from that, look!" He lifts one foot in the air, Cornwall clinging helplessly on. "She'll kick like a horse, remember that."

Seeing Edgar, the ape bounds over, coming so close that he can smell its fetid breath. Edmund, observing his pet, looks around in sudden fear. On seeing Edgar, he smiles in a friendly way.

"It's Poor Tom," he says affably, pushing the Dukes aside to get up. As he rises they tumble back onto the ground, fumbling at each other's trousers.

"Tom's a cold, is he?" says Edmund in the same voice, landing the Dukes a vicious backward kick. "Tell me, poor Tom, or should I say, brother Edgar, ha, ha, are you another who has fallen under the spell of the fair witch? I mean the whore, Cordelia. She who lords it over us as if she were not made out of ordinary flesh, like this," he pinches his own arm, "but some angelic substance. Oh, she's better than all of us. She's so nice we're not allowed to hate her even." His face is beginning to grow red, his tone strident.

"Lear has lost his wits to his lust, uses her for his piggery, and has completely given over his authority to her. She rules the court, make no mistake, don't let her silver voice deceive you."

He looks at Edgar with sudden cunning.

"Curan and Extra crowd over her like piglets over the sow, flies over the meat."

He gives a long, sharp sniff, ripping open his shirt. The eagle blinks out at the forest.

"She thinks she can put the curse of her eye and her mincing voice on me, Edmund!" He laughs harshly. "I'm not some silly underage courtier or doting fool to go fumbling under dresses. She's a whore as you well know, scraped from the bottom of some flophouse Lear woke up in one morning, wondering how the fuck he got there. That was before you joined up. She was so done over she could barely bleat her own name." He flings his head from side to side in girlish imitation. "But she knew how to use her mouth, no doubt about that." In case Edgar has missed the point, he purses his lips and makes obscene sucking noises. The Dukes giggle but Edmund ignores them.

"Every night she has the old lecher on his knees. He's gone beyond caring about the Sickness. He thinks he and Cordelia are charmed by the grace of God. The old fart's gone senile."

It seems to Edgar that the tattooed bird has grown bigger; its eye sharp and angry, bent upon him.

"He'll dote on her 'til she sucks him blind," Edmund hisses, drawing out each word for full effect, curling his lips back from his teeth.

Caliban has meanwhile circled around behind Edmund and is rubbing up against him, giving himself an erection.

"Fuck off," Edmund snarls, and turns back to Edgar again. "So what about you, Poor Tom, noble brother Edgar? Surely you have no cause to love her?"

His hand hovers over his pocket. The Dukes grow still.

"*Edgar I nothing am,*" Edgar says.

Assuming their conversation has run its course, and having fixed the stage back into his sights, Gloucester sets out again, only to find the dwarf still in his path.

It's not good enough, Gloucester," Kent screams in a shrill voice. "I won't have it!"

Gloucester looks down at him benignly, but with growing impatience. Pre-performance nerves are one thing; this sort of harassment quite another.

"Gloucester!" he yells wildly, as if at someone in the far distance, "Regan has a speech which goes:

To have her gentleman abused (that's Oswald, right?) *For following her affairs. Put his legs in.* No. *Put in his legs.* Then she says, *Come my good Lord, away. My sister may receive it much worse.*

She is not talking to you, Gloucester. You are not her good lord. So don't leave the stage. Stay on the fucking stage! Are you tracking me?"

In fact Gloucester has ceased tracking Kent's wild, confused words.

They remind him of something he'd rather forget. He sees Regan bending over him and hears her say, "*One side will mock the other; the other too.*" One eye has just been plucked out. The other is about to go. From here, right here, the terror springs. His mind slides over the scene. Kent has his stocks. Gloucester has his eyes plucked out. Equal justice for all.

Why dwell on such things? What is Kent trying to make him do; what secret hostile purpose does he have? There is terrible danger in sympathising with Kent. Offering him comfort in the stocks. Why doesn't Gloucester, Shakespeare's Gloucester, realize that? Why does he persist in his stupid loyalties?

The Fool appears, as he is wont to do when he is not welcome, and puts his head close to Gloucester's, resting his head on the Earl's shoulder in fact; pulling such a face that his lips hang almost to Gloucester's coat.

"*All that follow their noses are lead by their eyes but blind men; and there's not a nose among twenty but can smell him that's stinking.*"

What can these gaudy words mean, wonders Gloucester. The Fool's eyes wide with a madman's stare, but his voice is rich and smooth, word and gesture fitted with perfect accuracy - Gloucester envies his apparently effortless facility - but never is a sensible word to be had out of the Fool. Gloucester goes to push past him. Things are getting crowded.

"Are you tracking me?" Kent repeats, searching Gloucester's face for some flicker of awareness.

To Gloucester, the Fool says,

"*Let go thy hand when a great wheel runs down a hill, lest it break thy neck with following it. When a wise man gives thee better counsel give me mine again.*"

What council, Gloucester wonders? Why is he suddenly the centre of all this attention? He yearns to get away, to shake free from Kent and the Fool and to complete his intended movement back to the stage. Somehow the noble Kent is the harbinger of disaster.

He pushes past them while the Fool shouts,

"The knave turns fool that runs away;
The fool no knave, perdy."

Gloucester has just located the stage once more when a staggering weight lands on his back and sharp teeth dig into the rigid muscles along the back of his neck. He lets out a strangled cry and tries to throw off his assailant.

Drawn by the noise, Regan and Goneril arrive. Goneril and the Fool hold onto Gloucester while Regan attempts to pull Kent, who is screeching like a monkey, from Gloucester's back. Gloucester goes down on his knees, while Kent digs his fingers into the material of his dressing-gown.

"Kent has gone berserk," Goneril observes in a lugubrious voice.

Regan leans over Kent and whispers in his ear, "You'll get your chance." Kent's grip slackens a little. Regan hugs the dwarf, repeating the phrase, and they remain that way for a balanced moment; Regan hugging Kent who in turn clings to Gloucester who bends double and groans. Then the dwarf slackens his grip and Regan pulls him loose, cradling him in her arms like a child. With cool fingers she strokes his forehead.

"I promise you," she whispers, "you'll get your chance."

Kent buries his head in her breast.

As Gloucester reels free, the Fool pulls him to one side; he sports a conical dunce's hat with a floppy tail attached. He shakes his head sadly from side to side and holds his arms out in a mute lament.

"*We have seen the best of our time,*" he says in a hollow, portentous voice, the voice of Gloucester himself.

"*Machinations, hollowness, treachery and all ruinous disorders, follow us unquietly to our graves.*"

"*Unquietly to our graves,*" Regan repeats solemnly.

We hold rehearsal in the church. All the cast are gathered except for the Fool, who makes his own rules but is always there when his time comes.

Edmund stands at the back, nonchalantly leaning one elbow against the dusty font, a conspiratorial smirk hovering over his lips. Near him, on the floor, sit the Dukes, Cornwall and Albany, their heads on each other's shoulders, their mouths hanging open, staring stupidly at Lear who has taken centre stage. Curan sits on the floor too, but well away from the Dukes, up near the old altar area Lear has designated to be the stage.

I'm nervous without Extra, who's sitting in a group with Banquo's children, away from the bulk of the players. I can see her hands plaiting and unplaiting Little Extra's hair. Fleance is trying to catch my eye but I ignore him; he's scared of Oswald whose face is marked by the Sickness and who is sitting behind them, apart again. Fleance is getting old enough to cope with his own fears, I decide.

Regan is sitting right behind me, very close. I can smell her perfume; the summer one she takes from her crystal phial, mingled with traces of her own heavy amber scent. If I lean back on my hands to get comfortable, her ankles come into view, parallel to my shoulders. Being a gypsy Regan won't shave her legs (at least that's why Goneril says she won't) and down near her ankles the dark hair is peppered almost as thick as a man's. I try not to notice it, the way the dark hair contrasts with the pale luminosity of Regan's ankles, but it continues to occur there, in the periphery of my vision. If I try to move forward, out of range, I encroach on the 'stage' and earn a mild reproving glance from Cordelia, who's sitting near Lear, to one side of the altar steps, facing us.

It occurs to me that Regan is doing this deliberately. To embarrass me. I can't help noticing that several of Edmund's grins of complicity are directed at her, and that this is something to do with me, with Regan provoking me. Is she doing it to amuse Edmund?

Goneril also seems to be laughing at me secretly, sharing some joke at my expense with Regan and the grinning Bastard. Regan makes it worse by glancing at me from time to time while stroking Goneril's belly, or moving her foot carelessly so that it almost brushes against my hand.

When she caresses Goneril like that I remember a carnival trick I once saw, in which a man made a magnet out of an ordinary piece of iron by stroking it with just such a motion, again and again, with a powerful magnet of his own. It was not a real trick, but the audience would clap anyway, just to see that lump of iron lift a heavy cooking pot.

Lear stands up before the cast and silence falls over the room. The only sound is the clacking of Edgar's teeth and that is soon silenced by a dig in the ribs from Gloucester who has chosen to sit near his dear son. Lear is about to deliver his pre-performance pep talk. I sit up straight and put my hands over my knees, concentrating, as Lear has advised, on breath control and banishing from my mind Regan's ankles.

Lear begins. "You call yourselves players, actors, on what grounds? You haven't earned the right, the privilege, of calling yourselves *actors*, for Christ's sake." To demonstrate what it might feel like to have earned that right, that privilege, he squares his shoulders, centres his spine, throws his head back and thrusts out his belly and chin. "Posture, posture. It all comes back to posture."

Edmund snickers and the Dukes break into a fit of sneezing. Regan's ankle moves a little closer to Curan's hand. Lear holds up his hand for order, and, at the back of the room, like an echo, Edmund does the same.

"In the past few performances there have been some dreadful lapses. I would hardly be worthy of being your director if I wasn't prepared to point such things out. We work towards an idea. The perfect performance. However far we fall short of this, we fall short of grace. There are simple things we can all do to keep the thing moving. Be onstage at the right time, get off at the right time, catch your cues," he turns on his old friend, Gloucester, whose back has stiffened at the mention of posture. "For a start you, Gloucester, are slowing down. Grinding through the lines like a fucking concrete mixer and petering out in the middle of speeches." Gloucester stares at the floor, feeling personally betrayed by Mainchance's remarks.

"I know you deliver your lines like a zombie, Gloucester, but at least you could get through them faster. Be a fast zombie." He nods his head at Gloucester who nods back in time. "Get through them faster, Gloucester, *faster, faster, faster.*"

Gloucester nods his head numbly in time with Lear, his lips pulled into a sickly grin. Why is Mainchance torturing him, after he has just suffered a severe shock? He nods so vigorously that his chin knocks into his chest. Curan stifles a nervous laugh. This is Lear's pre-performance winding up of Gloucester. They have seen it before and will doubtless see it again before the show begins.

Edmund yawns hugely behind his hand.

Lear turns back to the rest of the cast, his eyes flickering to the back of the room where, in the semi-darkness, Edmund is watching him.

"If Gloucester is a problem," he resumes, "The Dukes are a complete washout. Missing cues, jumping lines, mixing speeches, giggling through horrific and serious events, wandering across the stage at odd moments, falling over props, carrying on obscenely, obstructing other actors - I could go on." He fixes the Dukes in his stare. "What you do with your personal lives is your own business. That's well understood, and part of the long and honourable tradition of drama. But on stage you have to perform, damn your eyes, that's why you're there, that's why your food goes into your mouths. You have to know your lines and get through them. Even Gloucester can manage that much."

At the mention of Gloucester, the Dukes giggle and tickle each other in the ribs while Edmund makes a low rebellious sound in the back of his throat. When Lear glances at him, Edmund turns and looks behind as if at some other responsible party, even though he is virtually leaning against the back wall. Lear resumes in a measured tone, talking to the Dukes but all the time watching Edmund.

"You Dukes should bear in mind that you aren't indispensible. You aren't even actors, for Christ's sake," his voice rises in pitch, "But a pair of cocksucking pillheads and a liability to The Shakespeare Company. A couple of clapped out circus performers who had some shoddy act and now think you can handle the stage." He turns to us. "They should bear in mind, these Dukes that call themselves players, that there are others coming on, waiting in the wings, already capable of taking major roles."

With this he throws a warm, open smile to Curan; a smile that abruptly opens a door to his youth. For a moment Curan confronts the person Gloucester calls Mainchance. She catches the smile awkwardly, with blushes, suddenly in mind of the low moans she hears sometimes at night from the vicinity of Lear and Cordelia's bed; she squirms around so much that her elbow gives way and she falls heavily onto Regan's leg.

A murmur of discontent runs through the players, or at least Edmund tries to rouse one, the effect being marred by the ragged and belated entry of the Dukes.

Lear peers through the gloom to the back of the church. Facing him across the dim waste is his ancient adversary, the Bastard Edmund.

"In front of you all," he says gravely, "Who are witness to my words, I accuse Edmund, at present skulking behind you all, of sabotaging the play, I mean the performances, and leading the Dukes to ruination."

He stops and allows the silence to grow heavy.

Edmund places his feet apart and puts his hands on his hips. When he speaks his voice rings out over the church, thick and churlish.

"I know my lines."

"When you choose to deliver them," Lear shakes his head vigorously, as though to release something stuck there. "Even though you haven't the slightest concept of irony, delivering Edmund's lines as if they were sincere."

This is not what Lear means to say. Somehow he has allowed himself to get sidetracked from the main issue, which is not Edmund's concept of irony. There are other antics of a more serious nature, God alone knows.

"Twice in the last performance, you, Edmund, tripped the Dukes up on stage, sending them sprawling over Kent, who was in the stocks, turning the scene into mayhem. And in Act V, when Edmund's humiliation finally comes, Caliban appeared, roaring and bearing his teeth in a horrible fashion, scaring Kent and Edgar off the stage and scaring hell out of the audience, many of whom left before the second collection."

"In the face of these things I have to ask myself, what sort of feel does Edmund have for tragedy? None. Not a whit, damn your eyes," he turns to us, making a strong appeal. "This so-called Edmund is nothing but a geek, the same ilk as his slaves, the Dukes. He is a thug, a pug-ugly, eager to smash anything larger than the narrow circle of his ignorance. At one time I thought I could make a player of him, now I face my own folly. Only an hour or so ago, on the wharf, Caliban and the brainless Dukes were called in to do service for their master, to humiliate Lear and destroy the presentation." He turns back to Edmund.

"We are all one step away from hunger. Long ago the cities and towns were looted for their supplies. Even now I can feel hunger for real meat pressing against my guts. When I close my eyes I can see stars and empty spaces. Do you want to eat royally, like a noble? Do you want to eat at all, Edmund? Do you want to suck on roast pig or nibble like a rat on a crust of bread?"

He appeals to Edmund now, his voice breaking into tremolo, a technique he uses effectively on stage.

"Even at the best of times a player's existence is a precarious one. The play is our only vehicle; it has been like this back to the time of the Bard himself. The play is our source and sustenance; if you pollute it, Edmund, what will the rest of us eat? Or find a bone to suck the marrow?"

Lear stops, feeling exhausted. None of what he has said is what he wanted to say; his words are full of heat but strangely without substance. In the aftermath of his speech he is assailed by the sense of loss and dislocation he experienced earlier. Edmund he can see, grinning at him like a death's head; between them swing pitted moons, vacant worlds, galaxies upon galaxies of them.

I have to breathe, he tells himself sternly. Nothing is more important than breathing. These feelings he is having, this strange dizziness, are nothing more than hunger for real food. Hunger can produce such sensations; light-headedness, giddiness, weariness, even hallucinations. That is what we are all suffering from, he realizes. Tertiary hunger.

Edmund's face has a mottled, blotchy appearance and his eyes are bulging from his face. There's a big discharge of energy into the room, like a burst of static. I expect to see Lear fall over dead but he continues to stand there, lost in thought, rocking slightly back and forth on his heels, his left shoulder pulled down as if under some heavy weight.

Edmund turns to the cast, an ugly look on his face, his voice choked.

"Why don't you realize that Lear is finished? Just like Gloucester. Gloucester is dropping lines faster than losing brain cells. Lear knows it. What he doesn't know is that the same thing is happening to himself, do you, nuncle? They are both a couple of fucking windbags, drifting further and further away from the reality of events. It is well known that Gloucester needs prompting all the time, Lear is travelling the same road.

"Sure, I'm pissed off," he appeals to our reason, our sense of fair play. "Who wouldn't be pissed off in a shambles of a company like this? Clearly, it is time for Lear to stand down and let somebody else take his role. Someone younger and more vigorous. There is plenty of room for him as an attendance or a soldier. Curan and Extra have a hard job filling in all the crowd scenes." He nods and winks at Curan, who has wrapped her arms around her knees and stares fixedly at the floor some distance ahead of Regan's foot.

Edmund moves into the centre of the room, his eyes sweeping across us. It is a clever move which pushes Lear off to one side.

"Who hasn't, at some time or another, cursed Caliban? True enough, the animal is not that easy to control, especially when he is hungry and excited. But isn't he also our protection? Who dares attack us when Caliban is around? Lear is living in a dream world where all the niceties are still being observed." He turns to Lear. "Do you even look at the audiences, nuncle? This Cornucopia of Culture business is a lot of bullshit, a pile of it a mile high. You can fatten any number of pigs on a pile like that, dream pigs." His voice shakes with fury. "The money we do get is because people have been amused, entertained, by Caliban and a few tricks. It is the clowning around that gets us the laughs, and the laughs that loosen pockets. Your tears, nuncle, and all that chest beating on the heath aren't worth a raw bean, if you want to know the truth; not a raw bean. Unless someone can get a laugh out of it," he finishes.

Goneril yawns loudly.

"I don't have to sit here on this uncomfortable floor and listen to this piffle, surely. I have only so much energy for rehearsals and performance. Right now I should be lying down doing visualisations or pre-natal exercises and generally taking care of myself." She waves an imperial arm. "Can't you men go and make up speeches to each other somewhere else, at some other time. Out of hearing."

Lear nods at her. Of course, of course. She nods back at him as if he were Gloucester. Regan gives a high-pitched laugh and puts her arm around Goneril, drawing her close. She strokes Goneril's face and belly, glancing triumphantly at Curan.

"There, there," she coos, "you can lie on me." Her voice is silky and seductive.

"I've done enough of that already, darling," Goneril retorts loudly. Everybody laughs, Edmund loudest of all. His are short, staccato laughs. Albany screams as Cornwall squeezes his genitals. In the chaos Regan leans across and whispers to Curan: "Meet me just on dusk, behind the church by the graveyard." Her mouth is so close to my ear the warmth from her breath tickles me and sends shivers down my spine. I refuse to acknowledge her. Or the pressure of her shoulder against mine. I can feel Goneril's eyes fastened on me while Regan hisses in my ear.

Lear bangs his stick on the floor, its brass knob gleaming dully.

"Edmuuuuuund!" His voice rising and growing as he stretches out the hated name. "I will make you a promise." He brandishes the stick at his enemy. "Before everyone here I will make a solemn oath. Tonight's performance will be a test. A test of your loyalty, the degree of your commitment, your passion. If you fail," he sweeps his eyes commandingly around the room, "you will either be out, banished; or take Oswald's role. Steward to Goneril. It is true Oswald has the Sickness, but he knows the play. He would make an excellent Edmund." Oswald smiles thinly. "And you, Edmund, would make an excellent Oswald."

The colour has drained from Edmund's face but he says nothing. There is another strange discharge of energy and Curan feels as if her ears have popped. Edmund is on the point of replying but checks himself. After an inner struggle, he bows low to Lear.

"At your service, my Lord."

After a moment or two of awkwardness we begin to rehearse. We run through two or three key speeches and what Lear describes as ragged entries and exits. The cast wobbles into balance and the rehearsal goes unexpectedly well. As if stung by the remarks of Lear and Edmund, Gloucester gets through his lines without too much hesitancy; only occasionally provoking laughter and comment with his habit of throwing his arm into the air every second or third line, regardless of its content. It is his sole theatrical gesture, often resorted to and sprinkled at random through the lines. Cornwall and Albany are shunted on and off stage at the right times, Edmund assisting.

Lear avoids rehearsing the scene in which Gloucester's eyes are put out, even though this part of the play has not gone well in previous performances. It is one of the few scenes in which Lear has made changes to the text, having Regan commit the atrocity rather than Cornwall, who is too incompetent to do any real acting. Gloucester invariably gets lost somewhere in this scene and has to be prompted line by line. Occasionally

Lear himself has delivered Gloucester's speeches from behind the curtain, requiring Gloucester simply to open and close his mouth. Lear knows how Gloucester dreads this scene and has probably decided not to add to his agony by rehearsing it.

News of Kent's attack on Gloucester has spread through the cast and Lear pays particular attention to Act II, Scene II, making sure that Gloucester understands to stay on stage until Kent has delivered his favourite lines.

As he watches them in action a sense of warmth and security steals over Lear. To act! That was the thing. To know the hour of the stage. All else pales into insignificance, and the whirling universe behind his eyes quiets itself for the pace and measure of the human voice; the steady rhythmic unfolding of the tragedy. Here is the essence of human experience, distilled and set down years before any of them were born, a play that could still find itself alive at the very ends of the world, in places like Babylon.

This, he understands finally, is why he is here. Edmund is wrong. Whatever the unbelievable odds, the Cornucopia of Culture *is* worth holding up, even in the darkest places. Such drama echoes, however faintly, the act of original creation, the explosion in which all the vast universe of forms was created.

Doom is there of course, he ponders. He can see it in the line of Edmund's back. Doom is inherent in every human act, just as it was in the original, divine act.

Of course there are problems in the execution, no pretending otherwise. Lear can face realities well enough. Human clay is malleable but treacherous; settle one issue, like the upstart Edmund, and another soon arises to take its place. There is no final equilibrium.

One issue of this kind is the growing tension between Regan and Cordelia. They can hardly be on stage together without some crackle of animosity. Lear finds it hard not to take sides. Whenever Cordelia appears on stage an Edmund-like sneer appears on Regan's face; she looks Cordelia up and down as she would a streetwalker. She can sometimes be heard echoing Cordelia's lines in a mocking tone.

For her part, Cordelia ignores Regan until she has to speak to her on stage, then her voice shimmers with emotion.

"*The jewel of our father, with washed eyes*
Cordelia leaves you, I know you what you are
And like a sister moth loath to call
Your faults as they are named."

As she speaks these words Regan eyes her narrowly, as one would some dangerous animal, tapping her feet impatiently on the stage so that they click mockingly in time to Cordelia's words. To Lear, a beautiful piece of acting, but not just that, for when it comes to her turn to spit out a reply, *prescribe us not our duties*, she does so with the greatest relish and vehemence, throwing her contempt into Cordelia's face. Cordelia's rejoinder is both a dark threat and a prophesy:

"*Time shall unfold what plighted cunning hides;*
Who covers faults at last shame them derides."

As she says these words her skin glows and her eyes grow larger, filling the words with such sweet bitchy insinuation not even Regan's half-lidded insouciance can match.

Edmund, who should leave the stage before this exchange, often stays as a shadowy figure in the background, eyes glowing, watching the women as if they were two rare gaming birds, prizes in a private menagerie: Cordelia in white with all the purity of a bride, her hair so often haloed in the lantern light; Regan with a sash of red around her waist and her full patterned, flared skirt and tumble of dark hair.

All of us share to some extent Edmund's fascination. Goneril, whose answer to Cordelia is longer than Regan's, draws to one side to heighten the confrontation. The rest of the cast grows still and even the Dukes cease for a moment their mumbling and pawing.

All and all, Lear decides, excellent theatre.

For Gloucester the encounter is filled with an arcane significance he can no longer fathom, although he is haunted by the idea that he once knew; that he was once a party to a more general and deeper understanding. The two women tower in his vision, larger than their roles. Somehow his fate depends on the outcome of this encounter; everything fraught with some frightful meaning intended for him alone. Are these Goddesses master of his fate that they should spit thunder at each other?

It was not always this way. In another world, another lifetime, one in which he had played the doddering councillor, Polonius, and discussed the shape of clouds with the moody Hamlet, the fair one was his daughter, bruised and crazed, who, not long after his own death joined him, the tresses of her hair floating out on the river; her white dress, the very same one she is wearing now, billowing out around her frail body.

Curan crawls across the dusty floor, taking infinite pains to make no noise. Her breath comes shallowly and from time to time she has to remind herself to breathe, to lower her diaphragm and let air into her body. Already her journey from the door of the church annex has taken an age; yet she dare not hurry. She can hear Gloucester, Lear, Kent and Edgar rehearsing the hovel scene in the main body of the church. Poor Tom's voice is raised in rasping song.

"*But rats and mice and much small deer*
Have been Tom's food for seven long year
Beware my follower. Peace, Smulkin! Peace, thou fiend."

It is not the rehearsal that interests her, however, but the low whispering of voices and odd sounds from the crypt, the opening to which lies just ahead. She inches forward, straining to catch a phrase or two from the clandestine voices, knowing without having to ask to whom those voices belong and what they might be saying, knowing she is a fool to be there, exposed and eavesdropping. Breathe. In. Out. Every actor must learn the fine control of breath, she can hear Lear say.

Now she wants to breathe without making a sound or so much as stirring the dust, and concentrate on the voices. Instead it is Edgar's voice she hears, raised in the madness of Poor Tom:

"... *that in the fury of the heart, where the foul
fiend rages, eats cow dung for sallets, swallows the
old rat and ditch dog ...* "

Suddenly Edmund's voice, low and distinct, "She'll wriggle like an eel in the pan, I know it." It is a half whisper, half croak, full of suppressed fury.

The laugh is Regan's, low and gurgly, possessed of a quality that brings out goose bumps on Curan's arms and thighs. More words follow but are lost in the noise of rehearsal. Curan has to ease further forward, risking exposure, holding her breath tight in her upper chest. Edmund's voice comes again, with an odd, breathless emphasis on selected words.

"If lips could taste a sweeter meat they would die from tasting. The Dukes will be wrung out and their blood fed to the dogs if they don't play their parts."

"Then dogs would die from fasting than lap that stiff flesh to sucking," Regan answers as if she is lifting something heavy and having her breath forced out of her. Their snickering mingles, but there are other, indeterminate sounds.

Gripped by foreknowledge and a compulsion to approach the stairwell to the crypt and look, and confirm, Curan eases forward. She can see down the stairwell into the crypt, a small space that might have at one time been used for storage. There is a dank musty smell.

"*Wine I loved deeply,*" Poor Tom drones, "*dice dearly,*

and in women out paramoured the Turk; false of heart,
light of ear, bloody of hand, hog in sloth, fox in stealth,
wolf in greediness, dog in madness ... "

They are directly below her, Edmund on his back, his shoulders on the bottom step, the lower half of his body on the crypt floor. Regan sits astride him, flared dress covering them from his knees to his waist. Her blouse lies crumpled on the floor beside them and Curan can trace the pale outline of her breasts.

The two figures are moving sinuously as if gliding underwater; periodically hisses and gurgles escape their throats, chained groans and swirls of sound. It seems to Curan that their bodies are being lit fitfully from some invisible light source, a projector playing a faint light show across them; globules of orange and yellow.

"Open the flesh at its tenderest, we will, lick the salt from the sound," Edmund says in a cracked voice, his head tossing from side to side, "Stuffed with leaves and the tongues of frogs. The bird must feed." It seems to Curan he is trying to rise against Regan's determined weight.

Regan begins to moan, beating Edmund's shoulders and around his face, hands flashing like ghost faces in the gloom of the crypt. Curan trembles. It is impossible for her to move back out of sight, so little does she trust herself to move without some clumsiness that might give her away. Regan shifts her weight forward, her legs emerging from under the skirt, calf muscles taut.

"She'll squeal," Edmund says fervently. "She'll squeal like a stuck heifer, I can hear it now." It is a distant sound, the crash of waves on a cliff, all-pervasive and universal, swelling in volume to a roar.

Regan emits a long, husky ululation, a sound foreign to Curan's ears.

"And what of the blushing one, the pretty Curan?" Curan blushes. "Which side shall the Courtier fall?" Regan hisses, drawing out 'blushing one' and 'pretty Curan' with vicious mockery.

"We'll take her either way. On her back." On this last word his voice becomes a shout, jerking his pelvis up and out, his lips pulling back from his teeth. Regan arches her hands above her head and bears down on him, her rejoinder lost to the muffled bleat of Poor Tom:

"Who gives anything to Poor Tom? whom the foul
fiend has lead through the fire and the flame – Tom's
a cold, bless thee from whirlwinds, star blasting and
taking."

Curan has a vision. She is flying through the air, far above the cloud cover, the stretch and curve of the earth beneath her. It is dusk and she can still see the flaming edge of the sun on the horizon. The cloud cover below her is tinged with orange. There are others flying with her, in formation; creatures with dark, leathery wings of huge span. She realizes they are not flying with her but towards her, up out of the clouds. When they reach her they go into orbit around her, eyeing her curiously. The nearest is close enough for her to see its face, dominated by a long beak and sweeping ridges of cartilage. There is a bleak nobility that stirs and terrifies her. As she watches it, controlling her motion by spreading her legs and arms, the creature turns gracefully over, spreading itself out to match her gestures, exposing its underbelly and genitals. It is a hermaphrodite with swelling, woman-like breasts, and a penis in full erection, while beneath the penis she can make out a dark vaginal opening. By the lazy, sensuous motion of its wings Curan is given to understand that she is being invited to mate. She wonders what it would be like to mate with such a creature, there in the air, its penis extruded into her body, its rough wings enfolding her, her head against its soft woman's breasts. As she considers it the creature begins to blur and dissolve, clacking its beak in annoyance and frustration; its head is no longer that of a flying beast but that of Edmund, lolling against the lower step of the crypt, arching his spine.

"Ripe as a summer plum," he slurs, as if the words were the wrong shape for his mouth. "Split in the right places."

A sigh is ripped from him by its own shuddering life. Beneath the floor of the crypt Curan can discern the fading outline of a flying creature. It is joined to another of its kind, and another, in mirrored series, pelvis to pelvis. As the vision fades completely, Regan skews to one side, half fallen off from the violence of his movements; the tattooed eagle rises up, its outlines flushes with blood.

Its eye pierces Curan to the base of her spine and I double up in agony, both hands gripped between my legs, my teeth ground tightly together to prevent me from crying out.

There is a movement at the back of the crypt. Caliban emerges, yellow eyes alert. Drawn by my sudden buckling movement or perhaps by some preternatural intuition, the animal knows I am here, its eyes fixed on the shadow that hides me.

I withdraw deeper into that shadow, back in to the protection of the rehearsal, a speech by Edgar:

"*How fearful*
And dizzy 'tis to cast one's eye so low!
The crows and choughs that wing the midway air
Show scarce so gross as beetles … "

After further rumbling, here's Gloucester's rigid monotone:

"*Oh you mighty gods!*
This world do I renounce, and, in your sights,
Shake patiently my great affliction off …
My snuff and loathed part of nature should
Burn itself out … "

"You missed some out!" Kent screams. He turns to Curan who's emerging from the annex. "You heard him miss some out," he appeals to her. "Did you hear the lines, *If I could bear it no longer and not* call, I mean *fall,/ To quarrel with your great opposeless will*, I mean *wills*. Shit!"

After rehearsal, Curan returns to the small tent set aside for her, Extra, and Banquo's children. As she enters Extra looks up at her guiltily. Little Extra is lying on the camp stretcher, eyes closed, her face resting on her arm, her long pretty lashes fluttering faintly to show that she is not asleep. The very sight of her fills me with annoyance. Fleance and Extra sit on the floor facing each other, a pack of cards between them. Everything looks normal but Curan suspects that Extra has been up to something with Fleance.

I don't care. What Fleance and Extra do when I'm not around hardly concerns me. I'm sick of them. I hardly know where to put myself. I sit down with Fleance and Extra and deal myself a hand, not caring what I play. When Extra crosses her legs I notice that she is not wearing panties. She studies her cards thoughtfully. Fleance looks at me out of the corner of his eye, but looks away quickly when I turn to him; the muscles of his cheek are quivering faintly.

We play in silence.

No time passes.

I get up and walk the short distance to the mouth of the tent and look out. It is some trackless hour of the afternoon. The air is heavy and slightly chill. The stage, fully prepared, is empty and silent; everybody is resting before tonight's performance. The fine mist that descended earlier has thickened and only a few ghostly forms of the forest can be seen. The day has entered a dreary, timeless zone from which there is no escape. I should rest but that is out of the question. I am tempted to go out into the forest but there are too many stories about it; stories about what happens to people who stray into it. I listen to the beating of Curan's heart. Thumpity thump. Thumpity thump. Too fast, like the sound of a rabbit on the run. Thumpity thump. Small feet thrumming the ground. Step on a crack you marry a rat. God bless you. A barge pulls out into the river, piled with corpses. Thumpity thump. Edmund arches his spine, the glistening sweat causing the bird's eye to gleam. Thumpity thump. Who is Curan? How is it I inhabit her body? My body is a skinny bag of bones. My breasts have just enough flesh to be tender. Thumpity thump. Where can I hide in Curan's body? Where will I find refuge, who will protect me, how can I learn to breathe?

The trees appear to move as I concentrate on them, shifting out of focus as if they are not quite where I think they are. I listen hard but cannot hear the sound of the river. Nothing moves but the shifting forms of the forest. We are at the bottom of a well with only a small circle of grey showing above. No stars, only the soft, pale light of the performance lanterns.

Nothing here to hold the eye, the whole place feels deserted.

Turning back into the tent again, I go to a small safe that sits by a plastic pitcher of water. I open the safe and take out some lentil cakes, stuffing them into my mouth one by one, hardly bothering to chew them properly. I'm not hungry. Not for lentil cakes, anyway.

Still chewing on the doughy cakes, I approach Extra. Perhaps she senses something in my walk, for she blushes. There's something in my stomach – hard, round and burning. I want to reach inside myself, into the emptiness between the bones and rip it out. Thumpity thump. I want to fly with the sky creatures, feel the fold of leathery wings. I stand in front of Extra looking down at her. When she looks down I can see the wispy hair that falls on her neck. Regan's voice comes, low and slippery, "And what of the blushing one, the pretty Curan?" Curan blushes again at the memory. "Which side will the Courtier fall?" Fall? Lear says that the earth is falling; the earth, the sun, the stars; falling through space at thousands of miles an hour. With no up or down. Who can believe something like that?

I swallow the last of the lentil cakes and order Extra to kneel and open her legs. As I kneel in front of her, I feel an aching down my legs and along the back of my thighs, as if I have been running for hours. Steadying myself, I put my hand up her dress, a white cotton design, flared to look vaguely Elizabethan. Her body is thin and bony, her slit narrow and hairless. I push my fingers into her a couple of times, feeling the hard, resisting muscle. Extra closes her eyes and sniffs as if she is about to cry.

No time has passed.

Fleance watches us curiously, so I make sure that Extra's dress does not ride up too far; anyway he has seen us do this many times. So has little Extra, who, I know, is watching us from beneath half-closed lids. Extra puts her hands inside my courtier's livery and begins to prod me where my flesh pouts, and a few light, silky hairs catch at her fingers. I concentrate on the lily and eglantine pattern on my blouse but no image comes. Sometimes I see a city golden in the sunlight; wide open streets thronging with people all jostling against each other; the beautiful theatre Lear talks of made of crystal, whose hanging chandeliers make a myriad of rainbows on the walls. The city has tall bronze and golden spires that chime in the sun. Sometimes I can even feel the sun, beating on my face. Today there is nothing, and when I open my eyes all I see is Extra's small pinched face, eyes screwed up tight in concentration. She pushes her hips down against my fingers. I believe I can feel her pulse inside her. Thumpity thump. Thumpity thump. Like a rabbit.

I push her away, suddenly very annoyed with her. The burning hardness in my stomach is still there. We turn to Fleance who sees what's coming but knows the futility of resisting, assuming a stricken look he reserves for these times.

Extra moves behind him and pulls his pants down. I take hold of his little member and rest it in my hand. A couple of inches of limp rubber, nothing like the somnambulant monster Edmund tricked me into seeing behind the wheelhouse. I stroke it underneath, along the joint of the flesh, as lightly as I would a caterpillar, while Extra digs her nails into his buttocks. His little scrotum goes tight and his cock begins to grow out from his body. He closes his eyes and grinds his teeth together. I am forbidden to suck his tube because of the Sickness, but I can roll it around in my fingers and squeeze it in my palm. Nothing else much happens; only once or twice have we been able to get it to squirt little globules of clear liquid, but I don't know what he does with Extra when I'm not around.

As I squeeze him, and run my other hand around his arse, I stare at Extra, trying to get her to meet my eye, to admit to me what we are doing, but her eyes are cast down, apparently fixed on the activity of my hands. I see her breath rising and falling shallowly in her chest, pushing her tiny buds, even smaller than mine, against her dress. None of us is breathing properly, I think with sudden fear.

When Fleance gets tired of it, he squirms around or begins to cry. This time I stop before he gets to that stage.

"Let's make him do it to Little Extra," I suggest to Extra, who doesn't look at me but nods. I can tell she wants to. Making Fleance do it to Little Extra carries our games to their limit and we have only done it once or twice before, and then with mixed success.

Little Extra sees us coming and pulls away into the far corner of her stretcher, as if that tiny space could swallow her up. I notice once more how pretty she is growing, her body full and round whereas Extra and I are thin and gangly. The sight of her there, helpless, fills me with fury. I hold her down while Extra pulls off the blankets and takes off Little Extra's pants. There is a set expression on Extra's face as she holds Little Extra's legs while I lift Fleance on. I position him carefully between Little Extra's legs, instructing Extra to hold them as firmly as she can. Little Extra watches with huge, frightened eyes and tries to pull away, kicking out against Extra while I soothe her as best I can, running my fingers over her silky hair and down onto her shoulders. When she has quietened I move one hand around between them, trying to fit Fleance's into hers; with the other hand I continue stroking her, softly rubbing her nipples to try and interest her in the game.

Fitting them together is the difficult part of the operation, and I am never quite sure if he has gone in properly or not. Now that my attention is divided, Little Extra lashes out, scratching Fleance's shoulders. He flinches from the pain, an angry look coming on to his face. I have to leave the more delicate task of joining them to hold down her arms. As I do this she squirms away from Fleance.

"Go ahead, Fleance," I hear Curan's voice saying, "Put it in, put it in." He gives me a peculiar, heated look.

"Pull her legs back, towards you," I say to Extra, with sudden inspiration.

Extra has her tongue between her teeth and lips, the way cats sometimes do without knowing. She renews her grip on Little Extra's chubby ankles and pulls hard, while I keep her arms and shoulders firmly pinned. Little Extra's pelvis is pulled down to reconnect with Fleance. Locking little Extra's wrists with one hand, I use the other to feel between them again. They are in the right position, Little Extra is quiet, momentarily exhausted, her crack moist and pliant. Fleance's tube is red and hard.

"Put it in," Curan urges again. A wild look comes into Fleance's eyes. He begins to co-operate and really get into the game, pushing and squirming up against Little Extra. She begins to whine. I take each earlobe between a thumb and sharp forefinger and press gently, in warning. She knows what she'll get if she makes too much noise.

Then he is in, perhaps for the first time ever. Little Extra's body has gone still and rigid. Fleance looks up at me, his mouth twisted as if full of food. Little Extra is breathing raggedly, the pulse on her neck fluttering.

Thumpity thump.

Holding down one leg with her knee, Extra feels up between them. "Let's turn her over and put him in from the back," she suggests, not looking at me, her lips shining wetly from where she's been licking them. "The way dogs do it." Finally she looks at me. "I saw Lear and Cordelia do it like that once."

"You did not!" Curan shouts at her, feeling as if she has been slapped. "It's a lie."

Extra pouts, which makes me want to smash her mouth. "It's not. I was on the barge one night. They thought everyone was asleep but I saw them," half closing her lids to demonstrate. "She was on her hands and knees and Lear was kneeling behind her. 'Turn it up', he whispered to her."

"It's a lie. You're only making it up," Curan turns away from her, viciously digging her fingers into Little Extra's arm, leaving white indentations with deep nail marks.

"If you cry out you'll get it," I say to her. "Now I want you to turn over."

"No!"

She fights with wild strength. Fleance gets off to help us. She is twisting and bucking as hard as she can, contorting her neck to try and get her teeth into my hands. I grab her earlobes and squeeze them against my nails; she goes limp and we turn her over easily. Extra and I pull her legs open until they loll over each side of the stretcher and Fleance climbs back on. He looks around at me helplessly and I see that his has shrunk again into a tiny, useless tube. I lean forward to slap his face but Extra interrupts me. She is pointing at something.

A thin trickle of fluid is dripping from Little Extra's slit, but there is something else, along the crack where her rounded buttocks meet.

Small whirled patches of flaking skin.

Extra and Curan fall over themselves rushing to the water, splashing their hands and frantically rubbing them with soap, not caring where the water goes. Extra looks up at Curan.

"Fleance was in her," she says with fright, "really in her."

They rush back to the stretcher and drag Fleance to the water, soaping him and splashing him all over. Little Extra sets up a wail, thin and high, her legs still limp each side of the stretcher.

"Why didn't you tell us!" Curan screams, turning to the collapsed figure on the stretcher. "You should've told us. You should've." The little girl wails even harder, burying her face in the pillow.

"She's got the Sickness," Fleance says tonelessly. "Maybe I've got it too. I'll catch if from her. Soap won't stop it. We'll all get it." His voice starts to shake. Curan leaps forward and slaps his face hard, leaving red welts where her fingers have marked him. I don't want him getting hysterical. He staggers back, shocked, then begins to yell, drowning out Little Extra with his brays.

Curan glances around the tent in a frenzy. "I'll kill you!" she screams at Little Extra.

Extra approaches the stretcher, a grim look on her face.

The flap of the tent is pulled aside and Lear enters, followed by Gloucester, Edmund, Cordelia and Regan. They all crowd into our little tent, suddenly filling it with giants. With one wolfish glance, Edmund takes in the scene, lingering on Little Extra still spread-eagled on the stretcher. He becomes aware of a high-pitched ringing in his ears.

Lear hardly seems to comprehend we older ones. He goes over to the stretcher and peers at the marks on Little Extra's crevice. Without speaking or looking around he holds out his arm to Cordelia, who, fishing in the pockets of her jerkin, hands him a small sealed plastic wrap. We have seen them before, and someone always carries them. He opens it and puts on two white cloth gloves, smelling of antiseptic.

Carefully he prizes the whimpering child's buttocks apart, bending low to examine the marks. Straightening up, he pulls off the gloves and drops them, with a fastidious gesture, onto the ground, turning to glance speculatively at Fleance. Without speaking he goes to the water and rinses his hands.

We all watch him, mesmerized.

"Now look at what's happened, Mainchance," Gloucester whines. "That's what comes of picking up children left by the river to die. If they are left to die, let them die. Death will find them in any case. We should shun children of the Sickness."

"Shun them!" Regan affirms. Gloucester looks around at her gratefully.

"We have the Sickness all around us," Cordelia says quietly, trying to catch Curan's eye. "Oswald, for example …"

"Yes, but Oswald's different," Gloucester bleats. "We know about Oswald. He keeps his distance from us and we keep our distance from him. Not one of us would touch his cup or bowl." He points accusingly at Little Extra. "She lives with us, shares our space. We dandle her on our knees and kiss her curls."

Edmund barks with laughter. He turns a leering eye on Gloucester. "Is this confession time, old man? Pawing her dress. Look to your fingers now!"

"Kiss her curls," says Regan dreamily.

But Gloucester has already turned back to Lear. It is a closed loop, he thinks mournfully. *I would have all well betwixt you.* Always it comes back to us. We can never escape it.

He says, "I thought we came up the river to get away from the Sickness, Mainchance. That was our main chance, you said. I remember. We all laughed."

"Did we, Gloucester?" Lear says in a disinterested voice.

"The barges were bank to bank, piled with stiffs. We gotta get out of here, you said. All of us agreed."

"Did we, Gloucester?" Regan says, her tone identical to Lear's. Gloucester turns to her, confused.

"You weren't even there then," he says.

"Don't take any notice of her," Cordelia says in a low voice, "And don't be deceived. The Sickness belongs to the wind. It blows wherever human beings go."

"Don't take any notice of her," Regan advises Gloucester.

"We thought we'd get away from it," Gloucester says to Lear.

Edmund says, "I hate to break into this but we're going to have to inspect the rest of the children. They might all be riddled. In fact, by the look of what's been going on here," he gestures widely around the tent, "they probably are."

"They probably are," Regan repeats, nodding sombrely at Gloucester who nods in assent.

Lear shifts uneasily. "What will it prove," he mumbles, not looking at Cordelia, trying not to look anywhere. "You can be rotten through with it and it still won't show."

"... Or it can appear a few hours after infection," Edmund says sharply. "It's our duty to inspect the kids. One of them might be covering up." His glance swallows Curan and Extra in one gulp. "They might all be covering up."

"All be covering up," Regan repeats severely, giving each of us a hard, glassy stare.

"We might have uncovered a whole nest of infection, right in our midst," Edmund says.

"Right in our midst," Regan repeats in an outraged tone. Cordelia starts forward and turns to Regan. A small animal sound escapes her lips as she bites back her words.

"I think this calls for decisive action," Edmund says to Gloucester. Lear looks at us with a puzzled expression on his face.

Cordelia says, "Do you think the children are the only ones capable of covering up? Finding a child with the Sickness is no different from finding one of us with it. I don't hear calls for a general inspection when one of us falls to the Sickness."

"Madam," Edmund turns to Cordelia with mock gallantry. His voice is mild and pleasant. "With due respect," he bows, "we must look at the children. We have clear evidence that they have been," he pauses and says with relish, "*experimenting*, bless them," he gestures luridly to the stretcher. "The chicken has been plucked," he continues, "the boy at least may be infected. And if this sort of circus goes on every day, as well it might, the girls are probably poxed too. We are their guardians. For their own sake we must ..."

"You choose your moment, Edmund," Cordelia says bitterly, "but I must ask you this: have these children been doing more than we ourselves do?" Edmund raises his eyebrows in mock outrage. Cordelia addresses Lear, her tone scornful. "On the basis of Edmund's strangely new-found sense of duty we should all be inspected for the Sickness. As Gloucester has just pointed out, she drank from our cups. We dandled her on our knees. We could all be infected."

She turns to Edmund, "You know," she says, impassioned, "We should all be inspected for the Sickness. On a daily basis. You'd like that, wouldn't you Edmund?" He inclines his head, his face a frozen mask. "They do it in some communities, you know. A morning inspection. It doesn't make any difference of course. The Sickness will strike if it is going to strike." She glances at Lear. "No human power can alter that now."

"I wouldn't mind," Edmund says haughtily, "I have nothing to hide. Nothing to be afraid of. I'd prefer inspections to having brats around with Death breaking out all over them."

He steps forward towards us.

"M'Lord?" he enquires deferentially.

Lear looks at us bleakly. There's nothing but icy space in the breath from his glance.

Cordelia steps forward. She has grown so commanding she seems to fill the whole tent.

"Let's just ask them," she says simply. "They can tell the truth."

Without waiting for a reply she turns to Extra, Fleance and I. This time she succeeds in catching my eye and holding it.

"Do you think you have any Sickness?" she asks us mildly.

I shut my mouth and shake my head, but Extra starts blurting.

"We didn't do anything forbidden."

Fleance begins to cry.

Edmund snorts with derision and turns appealingly to Lear.

"It wasn't my fault!" Fleance screams. He starts attacking me, flailing his fists. Edmund catches him up. His strong wiry fingers snip around the boy's wrists. He grins his big Edmund grin at me.

"Inspect them!" Gloucester says hollowly. "We've got enough to deal with already."

Lear glances at Cordelia who withdraws, pursing her lips into a thin, anxious line.

He waves his stick in our direction.

"Take off your clothes," he orders. I step forward; Curan will find her tongue. I look straight into Lear's face.

"I am not a child."

Regan claps.

The men take the blubbering Fleance out to be stripped while Cordelia and Regan inspect Extra and I.

"I put it in her," Fleance sobs as they take him through the flap. "They made me do it!" he shouts.

Regan glances sharply at me.

"They made me do it," she says mockingly.

"Let's get this done," Cordelia says brusquely to Regan. "They've been humiliated enough."

Her cool fingers on my skin are trembling as she helps me off with my blouse. I notice with embarrassment that my nipples have grown small and hard. It is not cold, rather close and damp, but Extra is shivering, hugging herself. I let my arms fall and face Cordelia, meeting her eye.

"They look fine," Cordelia says in a brittle voice, barely glancing at us. "No worse than a bit underfed."

"That's the truth," Regan says as she moves behind us, pretending to look for signs of the Sickness. She kneels behind me and parts my buttocks.

"This is often where the sores begin," I hear her say. "They climb from here up the back, across the scalp and onto the face. Only then do they move down the chest to the genitals. If the sufferer is still alive, that is."

"Very interesting," Cordelia says drily, her nails digging into her arm. "Have you finished peering up their bums?" she asks in the same voice.

"Peering up their bums," Regan repeats thoughtfully. At the same time I feel a light touch on my anus. I go perfectly still. Extra has touched it many times, usually accidentally in her fumbling, but this is different; firm and deliberate with a subtle pressure that is open-ended and full of implication. I can hear the blood in my ears, thumpity thump, like the swishing of skirts.

I can feel Extra's eyes on me.

A sudden screeching noise, like a distraught cat. Regan's fingers scratch me as she is flung to one side. Welts come up on my thighs. A glimpse of Regan's fingers dementedly clawing the air.

The two women are at each other, screaming and scratching. Regan goes for Cordelia's eyes, as well as raking with her feet as if she had talons. Cordelia shoves her elbow into Regan's mouth and pushes it deeper and deeper. Both scream shrilly at each other, whirling in a frenzied circle.

Enter Lear and Edmund who, after a moment's confusion, pull the women apart, Edmund gripping Cordelia in his powerful arms, eyes alight with excitement. Cordelia wrestles against him, kicking backwards at his shins. Edmund avoids her feet, grinning and pretending to do a little dance; grinning at Extra and me, at our nakedness. We move to cover ourselves as quickly as we can.

"What's going on?" Lear shouts, red in the face. "What new holocaust?" In the depths of space a green planet makes a lazy arc around its sun.

"She was feeling them up," Cordelia spits, lips twisted in distaste, wrenching herself free of Edmund.

"Feeling them up," Regan mimics, her voice going low and sour, twisting her lips at Cordelia.

Edmund laughs. "Girls, girls," he says in a jolly, reproving voice.

Lear approaches them, his stick held in front of him talismanically. He waves it in front of him, as if it were a wand and he could conjure words; to turn them all around, to wash them all clean of their pettiness and stupidity. He watches the stick with wide, fascinated eyes.

"Don't you understand?" His gesture includes all of us. "Tonight we perform!"

This is the sort of material I have to deal with, he thinks. These are the sort of people I have to weld into a cast. Somehow.

Ignoring the pitiful terrors of the heathlings, Oswald slips into the tent. He can tell them a thing or two but now is neither the time nor the place. Anyway, who would listen to him, Oswald the despised? Quietly he approaches the stretcher and kneels down.

Little Extra still lies where she has been left. Her eyes are open but she doesn't acknowledge him. Gently he lifts each leg and places it back on the stretcher, then folds the blanket across the prone form. Moving up to her face, her pulls the hair back from her eyes and mouth, touching her tenderly on the cheek. Little one, little one. Oh these human beings, these heathlings, they are too clever; far too clever by half.

At his touch her eyes move, swivel around to him. He smiles at her with his eyes, reveals his disinterested sorrow. Bends down and picks her up. She is staggeringly heavy but thank God he still has the strength to do this. As he raises her she burrows into him, nestling her head in his shoulder. He kisses her hair softly, cradles her in his arms.

As long as their short lives last may she never come to harm nor have harm come to her, he prays. Harm enough has already been done. For as long as he has strength, let that strength be in her service. What need has Oswald of that strength now, but for her?

May she see before she dies, some human love. Even in this world. Some human love.

Even in Babylon.

Exhausted, Curan returns to the tent, stuffs another lentil cake into her mouth and flops down on the stretcher, vaguely noting that Little Extra has vanished. She is glad Extra and Fleance haven't returned to the tent, and is not interested in where they might have gone. She is finished with them now. Her childhood is over; it ended when the tent crowded full of adults.

At last she has a chance to be on her own; to lie down and rest.

From her earlier feeling that no time was passing she now cannot hold back the headlong flight of moments. She is panting hard. She has to do something to get a grip on herself or she'll fly to pieces, scatter to the four winds, be dragged down some howling voice.

Instead she concentrates on her breathing, her actor's training; letting her body go loose and allowing her breath to find a deep and even pitch.

First she allows her diaphragm to fall and her rib cage to fill with air, listening to the sound of it whistling past her throat, imagining the wash of waves against the shore and allowing her throat to become loose and open, following her breath down into her chest, feeling her chest rise and expand as the air flows in; then releasing it and allowing it to wash back out of her, through her nostrils, a regular and even movement.

She is to make herself a tunnel for air, taking in what she needs and expelling what she doesn't need; carbon dioxide; toxins; accumulations; tension. Another breath. And another breath. She wants to connect each breath with the next; to form a long undulating chain of breaths. To become that chain and rise on a gentle swell of breathing. In through the nose and out through the feet. Nothing to impede it. Regular and even.

She doesn't have to do anything, go anywhere, stir her body into action. So her body doesn't have to do anything or go anywhere. Not yet. She can direct her breath into her stomach and the lower parts of her body, allowing it to release any knots of tension there. Her breath is a cool wind. She can direct it to wherever she wants, becoming more and more relaxed with each breath, letting her breath spill down through her legs and feet, letting her mind rise on the gentle tide of breathing. In through the nose and out through the feet.

She is able to visualize her internal organs; heart; lungs; stomach; pancreas. She can imagine what her body looks like on the inside, as if a powerful light is shining through her flesh, exposing the blood vessels, the muscle, the tendons, the nerve network, the bone. Her body is luminous, transparent. A vehicle for breath.

She can go with her breath, out through her feet, leave her body pale and inert on the stretcher and float upward with nothing to hold her down, up beyond the low, heavy ceiling of cloud and into the empty sky with its marvelous porcelain blue. There are no flying creatures to pursue her now, no invitations to mate. The sky is bare and without context; a great horizonless city spread out before her.

Now she can really breathe and be with that breath. Breathe with the breathing of the earth, the breathing of the stars and the seething place between. Breathe until she becomes breath itself; isotropic and universal. Life is breath.

All this she can do, but today there is no rest for Curan, however pleasant it is to visualize it all. She tosses on the stretcher, unable to relax or get comfortable. She can hear her breaths as separate, contingent events, but she cannot connect them up, cannot make of them a single event. Cannot become her breathing and so part of the breathing of all things.

Rather, the flat air sticks in her chest and swirls nebulously back and out again, full of dusty violets and reds, not even touching the tensions in the backs of her legs and thighs. On the in-breath she seems to be inhaling soot, some thick unhealthy substance that doesn't clean her blood or revitalize her cells. She has to fight down the sensation that she is not getting enough air, that the air is too thick and viscous to pass her throat.

On the out-breath, and the pause at the end of the out-breath, twisted shapes float into her vision. She sees Little Extra writhing and bucking desperately trying to cover the flaky patches; Regan and Cordelia swirling in battle so fast they merge and become indistinguishable; Edmund crooning and stroking the wings of his tattooed bird; the arching spires of the city; a barge of corpses; a creature with enormous leather wings circling the air, haloed in gold from the setting sun. And, finally, Lear's face filling out the whole perceptual field, his lips moving in silent speech, his agonized eyes fixed on her:

"You do me wrong to take out of the grave:
Thou art a soul in bliss; but I am bound
Upon a wheel of fire, that mine own tears
Do scold like molten lead."

It is hours since she has taken an in-breath. She lies soggy, heavy with the substance of the earth. Her eyes crawl down the sides of her face; her nose splits in half and she has to claw open her rib cage to let the air in once more. To again climb the steep, uneven slope of the in-breath.

A young man with black glossy hair and lustrous skin is stroking her, murmuring to her soothingly. She panics, fighting against him, fighting for the next breath. The air is filled with thick, heady incense. How much time has passed? How long until dusk?

Regan is coming towards me out of the dark. A shape that detaches itself from the shadowy bulk of the old church and approaches me between the sloping gravestones. She stops just long enough to touch my hand and give me a dark glance before moving on, beckoning me to follow. Suddenly afraid of being seen, I walk behind her stealthily. I can hear low voices from the church and backstage. Thumpity thump. In the gloom only the white of her blouse is visible, the dark, flared dress being lost in the shadows. Visible also, the pale curve of her neck, floating it seems, on some invisible vehicle that glides her smoothly along. The gravestones glimmer as she goes past, a faint luminosity.

Keeping just that far ahead, she leads me out of the graveyard and towards the river. Not down the mournful 'main street' but along a narrow path that skirts behind the huddle of shacks we call Babylon; gliding smoothly, turning to look neither back nor to the side, as if she has taken this path many times. Keeping the white blur of her blouse in sight, I feel my own feet padding clumsily beneath me, occasionally catching on a root or stone.

Sometimes she pauses, allowing me to close the distance a little, but then she is off again, a sliver of light slipping between the shadows. A glimpse of a profile.

The path takes a gentle curve into the forest, sheering away from the river. As the forest closes in behind us I try to focus on a particular branch, trunk or leaf, but they elude me. The forest seems able to change its shape even as you look at it; any particular point defying the eye, appearing solid only in peripheral vision.

Finally she stops in a small clearing and waits for me to catch up. We are on the edge of a small glade, a well-defined circle covered in springy grass. As my breath evens out I try to observe Regan without her seeing me. She is different here; smaller, lighter, taking no notice of me but gazing sombrely at the clearing. We remain this way for some minutes but still she does not move. There is an intensity in her posture, a stillness. A waiting. The silence grows huge around us. I would like to speak but my mouth has grown too dry. Any words that begin to form in my mind vanish before I can catch them.

I find I am still as she is, holding that stillness along with her. I am waiting. Not even waiting. Listening. Not even listening.

There is an abrupt shifting of the shadows around us and a sudden illumination. I hear Curan give a cry of amazement. It takes me a moment to register what has happened, what the sudden deepening and darkening of the shadow means. And why the forest is full of silver fish.

Moonlight.

The glade is bathed in moonlight.

Involuntarily I look up and see the moon, fleeing across a break in the clouds. The clouds shred and part before the moon like waves from a prow. I can't remember when I last saw the moon. Weeks. Months. Perhaps years. The moon and stars have become largely myth. I look back from a suddenly dizzy perspective at an endless journey upriver beneath a permanent cloud cover. Before that, nothing, nothing but a small child watching a barge loaded with corpses floating out into the river, turning slowly in the current.

Simultaneously I become aware that the bulk of the forest is still hidden and that Regan has moved closer to me. It appears that only the area around us is moonlit, the small glade. Regan's arm brushes against my side.

"Only here," she says in a hushed, reverent voice. "This is one of the magic places. A special place where the moon will shine if it favours you."

Favours me? I study the ancient patched and broken surface mankind once knew so well. How can it favour me?

"Haven't you been there, flown there?"

I look at her, confused. Suddenly the image is in front of me, as if her words have jogged my memory. I am flying across a bleak, airless surface pitted with craters bounded by impossibly steep, jagged mountains; in the sky hangs an orb, oppressively luminous.

Regan gives a low, vibrant laugh.

"Our ancient stamping ground. Actually it is not shining for us at all. It shines here in this fairy circle, and in others like it, for the little people who come to be healed from the Sickness."

Perhaps she senses my puzzlement, for I still have not spoken nor can will myself to speak.

"The wild is full of fairy rings now, Curan, just as it once was. Magic is coming back into the forest and the forest is returning with a hard salt in its veins, a bitter miracle. The earth does not forget. Everything that has happened is stored in its mineral flesh. All around us the old earth is coming back to life in new forms. Our human reality is only a small, oscillating fragment of this new order. The Sickness has touched the forest but has not killed it. Now it returns, and with it the little people, bearing their sorrow and the knowledge of their near extinction." Her voice has grown light and young, not much more than a child's voice, full of wisdom and wonder.

"They also bear the Sickness, but not as heavily as human beings. As the humans die off, and we are among the last, the little people and their kind return to claim what was once theirs, repossessing the land and jostling with the newcomers, for there are new creatures on earth, Curan. Creatures men can only guess at."

Again she divines my bewilderment, laughing, but this time in a light, high voice. I hold myself very still as she talks, trying to contain or at least minimize the clumsiness of my body.

"That is the knowledge of my people. They teach it to us as children when the campfire burns low and the owl comes down from the stars and the candle flame leans away from the shadow. They teach it to us with the ways of our people and the dream of freedom. When the last human being dies there will still be a gypsy left to walk the face of the moon. That's a saying I learned as a girl when the Sickness was deep among us and despair haunted our people. In the dust of the moon you will find the footsteps of the gypsy. This knowledge I hand on to you, Curan, and much more I can teach, for my people have returned to their long home."

"Is this knowledge open to all?" I ask, finding my tongue.

"Except to the men whose hands are locked and who can walk only one way."

I bend down and examine tiny flowers bordering the glade.

"Can you teach me knowledge of herbs?"

"The ancient knowledge has gone down with the sun. There was a generation whose teeth burned right out of their mouths and who died of starvation. The herbs themselves are changing. Many no longer recognize human blood, and have asserted their ancient prerogative to be invisible to human eyes."

"Yes, Curan," she chants, "there are newcomers to the ancient paths of earth. Hidden to human eyes as the little people are, yet known to us. They walk their own ways and have their own destinies." She pauses, moving her arm faintly against mine. She has closed her eyes and her face has assumed the emblematic appearance of a mask.

"Hear, Curan, the wisdom of our people, for it is also your inheritance. The moon will shine in the forest if you know where to look for it. And you will know where to find it if you lose your eyes and listen to your feet. The little people gather in such places as this, for the moon heals them and makes them strong again; when they have found their strength they will once more assume the mantle of the world. This mantle they will wear with grace and love. Miracles will happen again on earth. The mind will waken from its long sleep; but for humankind it will be too late.

There are no footholds for us here.

"Listen! The roots of the new forest go deep. Can you hear them?" she cups a hand over her ear and listens intently. "They go deeper even than the poisons men spread over the soil. Some go down so far they tap the warm places of the earth, where the mother broods over her fire, for the nourishment they seek. From these warm pure places the new folk drink, milking the sap. No human being could stomach that food." She is rocking back and forth; I would think she has forgotten me but for the arm that brushes mine as she moves.

Holding a flower between my fingers, I recognize the construction from Curan's vision earlier in the day and my hands begin to tremble. Each flower has a long stem capped by a wheel from which hang delicate crystals like chandeliers.

"I saw these today," I say suddenly, surprising myself. I have never told anyone about my visions. Not even Extra. Especially not Extra. "At the top of the stairs, by the wheelhouse," I add, thinking how out of place the old *Earl of Southampton* would look floating by these trees.

In my vision the flowers were large, as high as small trees. The crystals hung down ponderously from them, catching the sunlight, breaking it into the colours of the rainbow. Here I see how delicately each crystal is shaped to catch the wind; and how the crystals catch the moonlight, refracting into a shower of tiny moons.

"With my eyes closed," I add, feeling that nothing I am saying is making any sense.

Regan nods rapturously.

"These places do not observe the rules of time," she says in her sing-song voice. "They are nodes, patches where the fabric of the universe has worn thin. Here time bends back upon itself, completing its own movement." She does it with her hands, swooping them out and pulling them back to her.

She bends over, her head next to mine, and blows the flower gently, sending the crystals spinning, flickering moonlight back over her face. She glances up, smiling mischievously, her dark eyes capturing moons. It is a smile such as Extra might have given me in our best moments; a smile of shared complicity.

"As I understand it," Regan says softly, focusing on the flowers, "Each of these crystals is a tiny transceiver open to quite a spectrum of wavelengths. The forest is growing itself a nervous system; these crystals are receptors."

Looking at Regan now, so earnest and scientific, it is hard to believe that she can be much more than a year or two older than me.

"The flowers, the trees, the forest itself is listening into our conversation. Do you mind?" She smiles with a hint of shyness.

I know this is an act of great cleverness on her part, adjusting to my level, not talking down to me as people do to children, but across to me from the adolescent in herself, lowering her voice into mystery. I realize she is a brilliant actor, able to assume any role appropriate to the moment.

We sit in the middle of the fairy ring facing each other, and Regan begins to sing. It is a wild sound in a language I have never heard, full of long sustained notes and unexpected shifts of rhythm and key. Her voice has become ageless, the product of a time long before this, or from the far distant future. It is a free and turbulent sound full of the sea and the wind, wild love and languishing nostalgias. I see a landscape without cities where green valleys meet blue bays. Tall shaggy creatures neither ape nor man but which walk upright and speak long dog syllables.

When it is over Regan translates. It is sung by the mountain flower as Summer nears its end. The days draw in and the wind turns cold. The rocks begin to sigh at night and at dawn. Each evening the flower follows the sun down behind the peaks and each morning it turns eagerly to the east for the first yellow rays. At last the clouds come and it can no longer hear the singing of the sun; bitter rain falls at night, and in the morning the tough mountain grass is rimmed with beads of ice. Yet it continues to sing, not for itself but for the seeds it has scattered, that life might awaken in them to rise when Spring returns. Having heard this song the seeds will never forget. The song will be locked inside them, to sing again when they have bloomed.

She casually takes my hand, examines it, and puts it by her.

"You see it is not just a pretty idea but a statement about how propagation works. If the flower does not sing the seed will not remember to awaken." She looks at her hands. "The hands of a newborn child may have no lines for its fate is not yet upon it, but when its fate is upon it the song rises up in it and the stars plough across its palm, it remembers. It remembers its doom. Already it hears Autumn, scrabbling over the rocks."

She leans closer.

"In the old times, my pretty Courtier, my people knew all the dances of the creatures and the beasts and the art of calling in their voices. Of all the races of man it was the gypsy, who had no home, who made his home everywhere and tracked and retracked the lines of his faith, who opened to the songs of the earth and the wisdom of the woman."

Our knees touch, bringing her face very close to mine. Her voice has dropped to a whisper.

"I come to these places not only to remember the ways of my people, but on the off-chance of hearing some of the songs of the little people. They come to dance and heal right here, where we're sitting. I've never seen them but the Fool has. Does that surprise you? He's even spoken to them. He says they are composing a long epic ballad about the passing of the human race from this planet. This epic will always be sung so that our reign will not be forgotten by the little people and their kin." She brings up one of the tiny flowers and revolves it in front of her eyes. "By means of these little resonators, or whatever they are, these songs get passed from flower to flower, travelling hundreds of miles. By pitching their voices crystal sensitive, the little people can transmit their songs over the whole forest. You can hear it if you know where to put your ear. The Fool and I came to a place like this once, just to find a song and listen. We heard a part of their great ballad. Listen."

She begins to sing again. This time so soft and muted I have to strain to hear. The individual notes merge into one another, like distantly heard keening; the wind passing through the strings of a curved, delicate-necked instrument. A song not made for human ears, pitched not too high or low for them but rather out of phase with our hearing. I feel that if I listen to it for long enough my spirit will be lured from my body.

Regan bursts into giggles. "Did you know," all throaty and giggly, a woman gossiping to a woman, "that no woman, or man for that matter, has ever done it with the Fool?"

I giggle also. The idea of the Fool doing it seems totally incongruous. Once I start to giggle I find it hard to stop. This is the way I feel when Lear lets us smoke the sweet herb he collects along the river. Regan writhes her hands in the air. They look like two pale doves mating. I giggle harder. I giggle at the moon, which never giggles, and at the palpitating forest. The doves land on my leg and do a quick dance. I giggle harder.

Surely Regan is the most amazing person in the whole world.

Sighing she stretches out her legs and I follow suit, propping myself up on one elbow. I can hear the soft whispering of the grass and feel the resilience of it against the line of my body. It is remarkable how comfortable it feels. Close to me, Regan takes up exactly the same pose. Her mimicry is perfect, and in her face I catch the shadow of my own mesmerized, fascinated expression. I giggle again, hearing it deep and throaty like hers. It would be easy to float out through my feet and up into the sky of stars; I have to make a conscious effort to stay in my body. I listen for the surge of my heart. Thumpity thump, I say to myself. Thumpity thump.

Clouds are still pulling at the moon. Small animal shadows chase each other over the glade and race over our bodies. By adjusting my eyes I can change the focus and it is we who are rushing across a still and dappled place. Suddenly I see something to one side of the moon, near the upper crescent, something squinting, impossibly remote; lasting only 'til the clouds have engulfed it.

"Venus," says Regan in a hushed whisper. "Goddess of toads and lightning," a giggle, "Death in life, a dream of the poets. It is her, the bestower of kisses."

I have Regan's look and my mouth goes dry. This Regan I have never seen before. A mysterious confluence of energies; a compilation; a being ancient in the flesh of her people. Her hands sets up a dance between us, lightly sketching the air. My hand joins her and they dance together, in and out of the moonlight and shadows, retreating and advancing, almost touching then pulling away; two five-legged beings at play. As they play, landscapes go by them, hills, seas, coasts. Between the two hands, arcing from palm to palm, a thin thread of light; something we are passing back and forth between us while on my palm a circle of flesh glows with warmth.

Her hand is brushing against mine. On the palm. The back of the hand. The fingers. Encircling me in a whirling movement. I touch back, my slender fingers in a dancer's leap. Land like a butterfly, to take off again at the same moment as she twists around to meet me.

The tension breaks and we both giggle. In giggling I get a chance to take a breath. Swiftly her hand skitters up my arm, over my shoulder, down across my collar-bone, and come to rest lightly on my breast. I can see the steady flickering of the pulse beneath and pale flesh of her wrist. Thumpity thump. Her hands flits from one breast to the other, pressing gently on me and rotating her fingers lightly.

"Edmund would like to get his hands on these," she says dreamily. I grimace with distaste. I do not want to be reminded of Edmund or the scene I witnessed in the gloom of the crypt.

"He seems to be fairly well occupied elsewhere," I say archly, moving my body fractionally away from her hand. I can feel the welts on my thighs where her fingers scored them today.

"That won't stop him." She begins her girlish giggling again and I join her. I realize that I am being manipulated with great cunning, and that, I am confident, is at my own instigation. Yet I'm tired of this giggling. My own laugh is becoming strange in my ears. I never realized what a stupid laugh Curan has.

Still giggling, Regan rolls over on her back and looks up at the moon, light and shadow leaping over her face, subtly shifting and altering its features. She puts her hand up to her mouth to stop her giggling in a gesture I have seen from Extra, an adolescent gesture perfectly executed. She comes up to her original position again, smoothing out her skirt, looking shyly away from me.

"How did it feel today," she asks seriously, "Feeling Goneril's breast? Was it strange?"

"It was lumpy because the ducts were swollen with milk."

"That's what she wanted you to feel."

I have difficulty swallowing. My body is long and awkward. She puts her palm almost flat against my breast, holding a steady pressure, letting the heat seep through my courtier's blouse and into my skin. She is still, as if listening to the inner life of my body.

"Have you ever felt a woman's breast before?"

I shake my head. It occurs to me that her palm pressed against me with the same precise tension she applied earlier when Extra and I stood naked before the two women, has become a channel through which her energies flow, winding through my rib cage and around my lungs and heart, binding her to me with invisible thread, meshing our substance in some manner not yet clear to me.

She takes my hand and places it on her breast. I push carefully, feeling the rich heavy weight of it under my fingers, feeling across its roundness for its shape and texture. She looks down at my hand, her hair falling over her face so I cannot see her eyes. I stroke the nipple through the fabric of her blouse, sensing its tension and engorgement.

Spreading her dress out from beneath her so that it flows between us loosely, she takes my hand from her breast and puts it between her legs, under the dress.

"Have you ever felt the way a woman is, down there?" Voice low and husky.

"I've seen women plenty of times. On the barge. Everybody sees everybody." I think of Edmund and his tattooed bird.

"I'm not talking about *seeing*," she insists quietly. "You can't see what I want to show you. You have to feel. You don't have to pretend you don't want to. Your fingers are trembling now, against my skin. You have to seize your courage and do what you want to do, what you need to do. There are no secrets between sisters at this court, Goneril would say." Then, sharply: "Are you going to fiddle with Banquo's Children for the rest of your life?"

Her words sting me and I know that what she says is true, but still I cannot move my hand or do her bidding. Her thigh is smooth and even under my fingers, and I can feel the springy hair of her mound resting against my thumb.

She leans forward until her lips brush my ear,

"*Tell me truly, but then speak the truth, do you not love my sister?*"

"Goneril?" I ask in confusion.

"No," she coos, "The fair one, the golden one, the pure one; apple of her father's eye," a short, cynical laugh, "his mildewed eye - the fair but still fairer Cordelia, light of the world. Don't tell me you haven't noticed her. You pant after her. You and that little thumb-sucker Extra. *So young, my Lord, and true.*"

Cordelia's tones exactly, emerging uncannily from Regan's mouth; the same timbre, pitch and cadence.

"Then poor Cordelia
And yet no so; since I am sure, my love's
More richer than my tongue."

After delivering these lines with a trace of mockery, Regan gives another short, unpleasant laugh.

"You can be sure of one thing, sweet Courtier, she'll never let your grubby little hands near her lily white thighs, nor your tongue anywhere near love's riches, if that's what you're holding out for. She keeps everything for Lear and buries his nose in it."

"Why do you hate her?"

"Hate her? I don't hate her. Oh no. You've got it quite wrong. Our fair sister is like the moon; everyone must dream of her at some time in their lives. Imagine finding the fabled rainbow trout in one of these stinking ditches that feeds the river, or in the river itself for that matter. Beings like fair Cordelia are throwbacks, heir to an age of magic where women ruled by stealth, and bound their men's eyes with sophisticated spells. To mortals like us she can only be a queen. Only a queen can walk the way she does, be the way she is. Only a queen could heave her arse the way she moves hers. When she walks, that is." She lifts up one leg to put her foot up on her knee. This makes a tent out of her dress.

"But enough chatter. The little people are near and we must soon leave the moonlight to them. Quickly, feel! This chance may not come again; the clouds will fold back over the moon. The owl will grope its way in darkness, rats will fumble in the walls, the river will bear us away before our make-up has been washed off. Feel."

None of my games with Extra, Fleance and Little Extra have prepared me for what I encounter as my fingers enter a mysterious aquatic region of sliding surfaces and rich folds; muscles curves with secret, silky hollows and promontories; filaments of nerve-rich cells. I think of Extra's hard, bony slit, and laugh. Regan's main opening is so deep my fingers cannot touch the end of it, and instead of still, resisting muscle, my fingers are encased in moist sponginess, a passage wide enough for half my hand.

My fingers go everywhere with a fumbling haste, wanting to touch every spot. Finally I begin to work more methodically, moving from the tight folded anus down the rim and slippery hollow that debouches into the main sheath; following the swollen lips around the curve of muscle and back out again; up along the infolded triangle to the small rigid place set in petals of flesh whose meeting is lost in the mound of coarse, springy hair.

Regan is making low, faraway sounds and a humid odour comes off her in gusts, unbearably sweet. I try not to draw too much of it into my lungs, knowing it has the power to make me hallucinate, but already I can feel an odd lightness behind my eyes. The moonlight pours over my shoulders and the forest dissolves into a shifting pastiche of light and shadow. Regan and I are on a small island in a pitching sea of black waves; nothing beyond us will resolve into focus except the moon, hard and bright-edged.

Standing around watching us solemnly are a group of tiny creatures, naked and two-legged, their faces neither human nor totally unfamiliar. Looking closer, I see their noses have a different construction, with flaps and what may be gauzy filters. Their eyes, wide and intelligent, are set far apart on their faces. The men have beards and thinner features than the women, who are wearing their hair long and loose. All are naked and I notice some physical variations, such as women with long shaggy hair growing on their legs and thighs; men with a mane extending onto their necks and upper backs. There is the same ridge of cartilage, extending from the eyebrows up across the top of the temples and into the scalp, that I saw on the flying creatures of my vision in the crypt.

Among them I can see signs of the Sickness. Some of them are covered almost completely in pale marks. Others show signs of mental distress and the short, jerky concentration spans of the last stages of the disease.

Most are watching us with serious, almost expressionless faces. One or two, however, are talking excitedly and gesturing towards us. Another appears to be holding a conversation with one of the crystal-petalled flowers. One of the women is holding a stringed instrument and strumming it, but I cannot hear any music. One of the men is peering up the wide expanse of Regan's leg. This one seems to notice that I have noticed them and points up at me.

You are having too many visions, Curan, I hear a voice say, very close to my ear. You'd better slow up a bit. Get a hold on things. I feel myself struggle, my body twitching, my hand jerking inside Regan. I am like a swimmer, reaching for the surface of the water. I sense another landscape hidden, like a palimpsest, just below the forest. I can see the city of gleaming spires.

"I can see through the world," I say to someone.

An intrusive movement out of the whirling dark, behind the tiny creatures, distracts my attention. Something beyond our small island is watching us. I catch sight of a bullet-shaped head covered in scales. An impression of massive density and blind force. When I look back to the glade the tiny creatures are gone except for one, a man whose skin is so dark it is easy for me to miss him. He is standing near my leg, looking towards me along the line of my body. I am immobile, the jerky movement ceasing as quickly as it began.

I enter a pause in the rhythm of things. The fulcrum, the moment between the out-breath and the in. The moon hangs suspended on a ledge of cloud.

The creature leans forward and touches my leg. Several things happen at the same time. The whirling ceases and our island returns to a simple clearing behind which the forest flickers in the moonlight; Regan is gazing up at me, lying on her back with me kneeling between her legs. As I watch, her pupils fly open, releasing quicksilver into the moonlight. A current flashes up my leg and through my finger; her hips heave and she comes up at me with a feral snarl, her tube of muscle clamping tight on my hand.

"Do you know who I am?" she asks after an interval.

"I think you're a witch," I reply, not stopping to think about what kind of stupidity might be coming out of my mouth. "A witch who's taken over Regan's body."

She laughs and strokes my face. The laugh turns into a witchy cackle. "No, no, Curan; you confuse me with my sister."

"That's why you claw out Gloucester's eyes." I continue, surprising myself.

"You're wrong. I claw out dear Gloucester's eyes because he is a stupid, helpless old man. For no other reason. Forget Gloucester. He deserves his fate. Think about me. Do you still not know who I am?"

"Hecate?"

"Listen, Curan, you little fool, my own Courtier, I am a queen. The last monarch of my people. When I am gone there will be no succession, for I was born barren; in me the ancient bloodlines come to an end, and for that crime I would scratch out the eyes of the world."

Suddenly I am afraid. How is it I am naked from the waist down? Who poured this dark wine into my cup?

"What about the little people?" I ask feebly, wanting to push her away. How is she is kneeling over me?

"They're already here," she says matter-of-factly. "Watching us. When we are gone they will make up songs about us to add to their epic. How does it feel to know that you will live forever in the songs of another species?"

I want only to cover my pale skinny legs and hide them from sight.

Lightly, with one hand on my chest, she holds me down; the other lands on my thigh.

"Don't panic now, you silly girl. There's more to be done yet."

The impression of a dense, reptilian presence in the forest has vanished but I can still feel the pressure of eyes on me. The little people too may have vanished; not because they are no longer there but because I can no longer see them. I have become defensive and skittish.

Her fingers rest lightly on my thigh, as if observing the territory, Regan sighs, and I feel the tremble of intensity in her fingers which suddenly leap, confidently, to the sensitive ring of my anus. My sphincter muscles contract, I want to draw back into the earth. I've had enough of this now, but by degrees I relax again, and as the muscles of my anus loosen, her finger, by virtue of its steady, gentle pressure, eases into me.

Still my mind thrashes about. I'm sure the play will soon begin and the others will be waiting for us, cursing and speculating. The theatre goers of Babylon, the literati of that great city, will have ascended the steps of the Crystal Theatre, their robes flowing behind them in rivers of royal blue and purple. Backstage in the make-up rooms, hasty last minute preparations are underway. A touch of rouge here, a dab of powder there, a grimace in the mirror - Do I look right? Could you tie me at the back, darling? Of course it will all go well. *Nothing will come of nothing.* Where the hell's Curan? And Regan? Don't forget the lines ... Gloucester will be wandering from line to line, muttering to himself; Lear will be pulling himself to his full height; *Every inch a king. Meantime we shall express our darker purpose.* Cordelia will be by the make-up jars, a finger resting across her cheek. Extra ...

A murmur, sweeping around the gallery, like the rustle of leaves,

"... concentrate, Curan," Regan is saying, "You have to be here."

"We'll be late for the play." How thin and young Curan's voice is!

"The play will wait for us. Time has no jurisdiction here. As long as you concentrate."

"What do you want from me?" It is a great mystery to the young Curan what Regan could want from her, or why her finger would want to weave through the silky hairs on my mound. What is there in my thin, defenseless flesh for her? Enough is enough. I go to push her away but my hand will not move.

We don't want to lose you, Curan, the voice I heard earlier says, very close to my ear. I am a small child again, walking along the bank of the river. Ahead are a group of adults, clustered around a barge. Instinctively I hide in the bush, knowing I should not be seen. Above, on a small rise, I can make out the wrecked body of a car. I climb towards it, overcome by curiosity, my breath sounding in my ears as if it belonged to another person. It reminds me of the rasping sound Lear makes during his dying speech:

'Pray you, undo this button: thank you, sir.
Do you see this? Look on her, look, her lips,
Look there, look there!'

"Are you afraid I'll kiss you?" Regan whispers.

I watch through the broken windscreen as the adults pile the bodies onto the raft; body after body until the raft is overflowing with bodies. A woman throws herself onto the pile, screaming at the top of her voice. In her hand a flash of something bright and suddenly a gash of red on her blouse. The adults loading the bodies hardly even pause in their task. They are little more than weary automata.

"You must not, it is forbidden. The Sickness lives in the body's juices." An adult kicks one of the corpses; it rolls over and stares up at me.

Regan laughs.

"Oh you superstitious little fool. Is that where it lives? Did Little Extra get it from kissing?"

I say nothing. I have no wish to think about Little Extra.

"And I suppose you think your fair Cordelia pure? So sound and sweet of limb? Don't you believe it. Lear has the Death, although he won't admit it to himself. She must have it. It follows as night follows day."

"That's not true!"

Regan takes her hand from me and straddles my body, her knees pressing into my rib-cage. She bends low and talks intensely, all the while stroking my face.

"There are some things you must know, Curan, before you get any older. You are living in a dream world, and probably very little of what you believe is true. No-one wants to tell you the truth because they are afraid of it. It is more horrible than you have been led to think. The Sickness doesn't always or even usually attack the body first, let alone show up on the skin. It is a disease of the blood and it attacks the mind first. The mind, my beautiful. Look at Gloucester." She swings her hand in the air just as Gloucester does when executing his single dramatic gesture. "Clearly a brain damage case, with Lear going the same way. Edmund is right about that.

"All Lear wants to do is act out his dramatic roles and fill his head with heroic thoughts; thus, in willful blindness, he infects his very own daughter. Only men carry the Sickness, darling. In their sperm."

The perfect rounds of her breasts hang over mine. I can see the dark areolas with their trace of wiry hair. I catch a glimpse of the beak of the bird on Edmund's chest sliding into Regan's flesh.

"What do you mean 'daughter'?" I push up against her, trying to ease her weight. "Aren't you getting confused with the play?"

"Oh no. They really are father and daughter. Old Cornucopia of Culture is all incest. That's why he likes this play. It's all suppressed sexuality and incest.

The wren goes to it, and the small gilden fly
Does lecher in my sight.

Cordelia knows of course but it suits her to say nothing. She's a whore. A slut. A grab-bag."

I want to tell her that I don't believe any of this, that she really does hate Cordelia in spite of what she has said. That it is she, Regan, that is the grab-bag, the slut.

Instead, I lift my head up to her breast and take one of her nipples in my mouth. At first I am afraid it is going to squirt milk, but silly Curan cannot keep two thoughts together. The nipple is smooth and ripe in my mouth. I begin to suck on it slowly, rolling it on my tongue. My body remembers this; my mouth remembers what my mind cannot conceive. I am swimming in close, warm water.

When I have sucked both breasts she wriggles down until the length of her covers me like a second earth. She settles her lips on mine, fluting them gently but firmly as they seal.

A thick sweetness begins to flow from her mouth, sliding over her tongue and dripping into mind. I resist it. I strain against her weight. I push up against her breasts. I want to force the sweet viscosity back into her mouth. I know it will act on me as a drug, just as her woman's scent does. Already my arms and legs are getting heavy. Curan doesn't care anymore. The concerns of the court are no longer hers. She is a small girl crouching in the lee of an abandoned car; a spark of light jumping between two crystal flowers; a song no human voice can decipher. Her body is a pile of rotting leaves shot through with worms. It is as long and as full as Regan's. She doesn't care about the river of sweetness flowing in her blood or the weight of the flesh. Throw it onto the barge with the rest of the corpses. Let the breath tear a hole in your chest, Curan, and escape!

She rolls off me and her hand begins its work in earnest, slipping into me without preamble. Again I think of Extra's random fumbling, sometimes hurting me, sometimes striking it right by accident. Regan's touch is confident, deft and sensitive. I spread my legs as far as I can to give her fingers more room. When I do this she grunts and eases her forefinger as far as it will go; softly, deliberately, stroking the entrance to my womb.

While she does this I slowly examine her face. The moonlight has frozen into the whites of her eyes, and her pupils have grown enormous. She is not the Regan I know, but the one she cannot help revealing; the hag who rides her gypsy flesh, ancient, greedy and unsatisfied. I don't want to look at her. Her face is haggard in its pleasure, the inside of her mouth is black from all the lies she has been telling me; her teeth are yellow and broken.

"What do you want?" I ask this ancient being. She is holding my legs apart with her knees, her hands beating a dance on my body.

Her mouth opens and closes soundlessly, as if she is underwater.

Then I get the answer. It takes place inside me. From the far corners of my body, a tingling response to the even movement of her finger; a trickle of movement and sensation in that direction. A slow twist at the base of my spine. All this gathers, moves blindly in concert towards her finger.

I turn my head to one side. One of the tiny crystal flowers hangs near my eyes and I see it as I first saw them, there by the wheelhouse, up close and large, the crystals hanging heavily from their wheel. Inside one of these I see myself lying, embalmed, in a posture of formal peace. I am old, my breasts withered and my thighs ridged with slack muscle.

One of the small creatures I saw earlier emerges from behind the flower dressed as Lear is described in Act IV, Scene VI - fantastically dressed with flowers. As she approaches I see she has long fair hair with shaggy down growing on her thighs and lower legs. Her features are generally human except for the nose, which is distended with the hint of a snout. She carries a stringed instrument, perhaps the same one I saw earlier, and begins to sing, sitting only a few inches from me, her voice high and thin.

Dancers appear from around her and begin to move rhythmically to her song. Two columns of dancers, one of men and one of women, sway towards each other with unmistakable sexual intent, thrusting out their pelvises and breasts. I realize I am seeing, in stylized miniature, the drama of courtship and love. The rhythm of their dancing is in time with the rhythm of the movement of Regan's finger, now moving easily in and out of me, sometimes withdrawing almost to the limit. I see her lips moving to the words the creature is singing. The dancers come together and move apart, stamping their feet; first one, then the other. I feel the faint vibration along my leg.

My body goes cold and slips off me like an old skin. I am reduced to a circle of heat, clamped tight around Regan's finger. She is very near to getting what she wants; the far-flung parts of my body lean towards her. All that she has summoned has gathered, a dense ball in my groin, awaiting her final command. The melancholy, alien song sounds distant but holds me here, gyroscopically, on the face of the earth. I understand that my mind, like the crystals, is a resonator, able to broadcast the song far into space. There, it is picked up by the stars, amplified, and carried to the far corners of the universe.

Regan increases the tempo, increasing the pressure on the upper side of my sheath. Then, with a short, stabbing motion she sucks me into her. Curan vanishes, collapsed to an extensionless point. I unravel into her convulsively all that is me and the secrets of my life, and she sucks it all in through her finger, her skin glowing with youth. She is a wild, exultant girl, not much older than myself. There never was any ancient hag.

As my body ruptures into hers I feel tiny hands laid upon me. I reach up and touch solid marble pillars behind me. Cordelia is lying to one side, wrapped in the arms of a lover. I see the lover she has chosen from among the slaves is dark and gypsy looking, like Regan; a hermaphrodite with the breasts of a woman and the genitals of a man. Cordelia smiles at me lazily. I look back at the figure who has just absorbed me. This is not Regan but a young man with black glossy hair and lustrous skin. From inside his face Regan smiles at me. The slave looks at me tenderly and pulls his body back. Something huge glides out of me.

"It is finished," he says.

Regan pulls her hair back from her face and back over her shoulder. Her face is clear and full of powerful command. She shakes her hair down her back and lets the moonlight fall on her face.

A shadow detaches itself from the forest and moves towards us, a ponderous shadow; the lurch of bulk and deformity. I start away in fright.

"It's all right," Regan says calmly, "It's only Goneril."

"..."

Regan shrugs and puts on her blouse. I sense she wants nothing to do with me, but I want to take her and busy my head on her breast as a child would; she looks serene and beautiful. I fumble for my own clothes.

As Goneril approaches I recall the bullet-shaped head and scales gleaming in the moonlight. An ungainly shadow falls over us. None of us says anything. Goneril sits down. Regan has withdrawn into herself and stares moodily out into the forest. A raft is pushed out into the river. Several bodies roll off and float beside it; mother and ducklings. A large black bird lands on the barge. One of the corpses sits up. An adult points towards the car where I am hiding.

I dress hurriedly, neither woman taking any notice of me. My body feels awkward and weak. There is an invisible bond between them I cannot share. A light breeze touches the forest; the flowers nod madly, their crystals chiming.

"You are a woman now," Regan says in a quiet, hard voice. "You will no longer sleep with Banquo's Children, nor with Extra, nor be forced to keep company with them. You will sleep with us and be our equal. I will groom you for the role of Regan; Extra would love to understudy for Cordelia."

Immediately, I look at Goneril to see how she is receiving this speech but she is lost in profound silence, her heavy jaw set in immobility. I ponder Regan's words. If I am to be treated as an equal, how is it that I'm still being ordered around like a child?

Goneril rubs her swollen belly, enclosing it protectively. The presence of this woman is inescapable, some hint of that density and laconic power I sensed in the half-glimpsed figure in the forest.

Finally Goneril breaks the silence.

"They hurt me now, these orgasms. The muscles of the uterus are so stretched."

No-one comments and the silence lengthens again. We each become a weight on some three-cornered see-saw, held in precarious balance. The world tips forward.

The moon disappears like an eye being shut.

As if it were a pre-arranged signal, some private deal between Goneril and the cosmos, she rises, talking.

"There is a fascinating story," she says floridly, "concerning two lovers. Since their courtship was forbidden by their families they had to seek quiet places away from the village to be alone. One day, having slipped away, they discovered a small hill, affording good clear views, and tumultuous roots amongst which they could lie. So they lay down and, having filled their cup with love to overflowing, they went to sleep.

"They were so close that in their sleep they shared the same dream. A fairy princess of extraordinary beauty appeared to them and promised them eternal life and love on the condition that, wait for it, they never opened their eyes to look at each other. I'm sure you'll recognize the double bind that usually accompanies the gift of the good fairy. Anyway, as may be expected, all went well until that fateful day they tested the prohibition.

"As soon as they looked at each other the dream ended and they woke up to find themselves aged and querulous, their beauty gone and the skin sagging from their limbs. When they realized their condition and remembered how they had lain down under that accursed tree in the first flush of youth, they began to wail and scream, turning on each other and accusing each other of being the first to break the fairy princess's interdiction, hating each other for their wrinkled and haggard appearance.

"Just then a little girl came along and enquired what the matter was.

" 'Little girl, little girl,' the two aged lovers said to her. 'Yesterday we were young, just a handful of years older than yourself. Our limbs were smooth and supple. Sunlight followed us wherever we went. We spent the night under this accursed tree and slept amongst the roots, and look at us now.' They thought it was unnecessarily confusing to tell the little girl about their dreams, and the fair princess's deal. Anyway, that dream was already fading from their minds and they only half believed it had happened.

" 'Lucky for you, you get another chance,' said that young girl, who was really the beautiful fairy princess in disguise, and with a wave of her magic wand she turned back the years and lo, the lovers found themselves back in their youthful flesh again! They looked around to thank the little girl, but she was already gone.

"As soon as they looked at each other they were stunned by the beauty they saw, forgot their quarrels, and fell in love all over again. Once more they lay down beneath the tree, amongst the roots; and once more, their limbs weary from love, they fell asleep.

"When they failed to return home their families became worried and sent out search parties. They were never found, but would you believe that to this very day, on that hill, beneath that tree, you will observe two upraised roots so thoroughly intertwined that one cannot be distinguished from the other."

"Are you trying to tell us something?" Regan asks acerbically.

Goneril bows. The tiny crystal flowers throw miniatures of her shadow across the glade.

Goneril says, "The players are assembled; in the balconies the gentry have taken their seats and the rabble press into the pit. Ladies," gesturing low with her arm, "the stage ..."

Re-emerging from behind the church where she has stepped just a moment ago, Curan almost stumbles into Lear and Gloucester who are deep in conversation. Lear is running his hand through his hair and beard, combing them smooth. He looks thoughtfully at Curan as she passes.

"The play relies," he says to Gloucester, "on a strongly presented, humanitarian Gloucester. You see, Gloucester's plight is not intended by the playwright, God rest his soul, to distract from the agony of the hero, Lear himself, the mad king. In fact Gloucester's trials are intended to reflect and augment the cosmic passions of Lear. It all contributes to the oppressive atmosphere of the drama; the audience is offered no relief. The sub-plot lands them in the same horror they have just been watching. You can read all this stuff in A. C. Bradley or Wilson Knight. I strongly advise you to do that, Gloucester." He spreads his arms wide and slightly in front of him.

"A great play like this walks on a knife's edge, and when you walk on a knife's edge you have to go at a certain speed or you fall off. Or you cut your feet. Pace, Gloucester, pace. Clip through those early scenes with your long rants about the degenerating state of things, portents and signs and so on. Clip through them. A steady canter. Clippity clop," jiggles imaginary reins. "Then you're home on a pig's back. A drama of this stature, in which the powers of light and dark so sharply contend, has a headlong momentum, a dreadful inexorable movement," he pushes his hands together, "a squeezing, a pumping."

Gloucester nods his head. Pace. Yes. The dramatic force of. Out of the frying pan and into the fire. His head moves reflexively back and there's a crunching noise at the top of his spine.

"I need a massage."

"The alternative is getting bogged down. Everything hinges on not getting bogged down. You get bogged down, the audience gets bogged down; linger too long here, stop to pick the daisies there, and the audience has lost you. I mean you've lost them. They start to talk and murmur among themselves, missing more precious lines, somebody makes a jeering noise at a moment of high tension." Lear wipes his forehead, "And the next thing a tomato comes out of the audience. Laughter. Rotting eggs. Disintegrating fruit. Bags of urine. Christ knows what."

Gloucester looks bleakly across the field. Already a few people have gathered, drawn by the night lamps and the preparations. These people don't look as though they will be throwing disintegrating fruit or bags of urine; their faces are blank and lustreless, their motions as abstracted as sleepwalkers'. They look as if they only half inhabit the world, Gloucester thinks. It's the Sickness. It's even among the children, the corrupt little brutes. It pulls us down. Drains the world.

"Listen, Mainchance..."

"Don't call me that."

"But I..."

"I am not that."

"But, Mainchance, I ..."

"Gloucester, I am Lear; petulant, aging monarch to some nameless kingdom."

"What I wanted to say is that I don't like this play. I've never liked it, if you want to know the truth. There's some evil in it. Can't we do another? Something with a bit of," he throws his arm into the air, "beauty. Something uplifting. A bit funny. What about *The Tempest*, I know how well you do Prospero. What about *A Midsummer Night's Dream*. Now there's a play! Full of mystery and magic! I played Bottom once and had to wear an ass's head," he grabs hold of Lear's arm. "It was all stuffy but I did get to lie down with the Queen of the Fairies." He faces Lear.

"I hate this fucking play, that's the truth. I don't want to read Bradley or Wilson Knight. Anyway, where would I get books like that?"

"In any university or college library."

"I can't remember any of Bottom's lines right now but..."

"What about Gloucester's?"

"I'm sure I could learn them fast enough, I ... " He stops, his hand suspended in front of his eyes.

"I can't see. Christ. Mainchance!" voice rising in panic. "There's something blocking my vision."

"You've got your hand in front of your face."

"Really? Is that a true explanation? My hand is in front of my eyes to test my vision. I am getting a selective blackening effect. It could be pressure on the optic nerve; I've got a frightful headache. That's relating to this pressure on the back of my neck."

Lear wanders off vaguely towards the stage. After all, he needs his strength too, and there is only so much you can do with Gloucester. You reach a limit. You admit that limit and you walk away. You need time to be alone yourself, before the performance. Don't forget you are the pivot of the whole thing. You need time. Time to summon, from your depths, that strange and irradiating presence that is you, Lear, centre-stage. The full mask.

Each time it demands a little more. Each time it is a little harder, the movement more sluggish. Words like 'irrevocable', 'fate' and 'avouched', crowd in his mind.

Lear, I summon you. Out of the dead and the dark and the demi-fleshed. I command and enjoin you. I, your sovereign Majesty. Come forth! King! Pull the curtain aside.

He lifts his noble profile to the gathering audience.

The sage! Once more you will have your time, know your hour, enter the true groundwork of your being. Feel beneath your feet the rude wooden planks of the stage. In this case, of course, the green of Babylon. Come! I know you yearn for the stage with something akin to homesickness. Like a lost lover you pine away to a shade; onstage you are fully yourself, one with the ecstasy and madness of being. Offstage, what are we actors to you but a distant, garbled procession? Something like being with Gloucester all the time.

Profile a little higher. Pull down the corners of your mouth.

Onstage the mysterious and inaccessible will once more be within your grasp. You know that don't you, old deceiver. You cunning old bastard. Once more you rise. I tempt you. I tempt you into the flesh. The stage light hurts your eyes; the applause some ragged tide. The evening air is damp on your face. The place you do not know, the stage you recognize.

This is your beloved craft. *The bow is bent and drawn; make for the shaft.* I am Lear.

Gloucester hears a voice behind him, low and quiet. It may be Edgar but it is probably Kent. The voice sounds sincerely regretful.

" ... and I'm truly sorry about this afternoon's incident. It was the frustration. It builds up pressure throughout the body and my body's too little. Too little for that sort of pressure."

In order to turn, he'll have to move his shoulders and the whole upper half of his body. A movement of that magnitude would seem too intrusive, too blatant - even threatening. Whoever Kent, and he is sure it is Kent, is talking to, he wouldn't like to be interrupted by the likes of Gloucester. Kent is making a confession, such as murderers make, and that requires a fairly intimate context.

It may be better for Gloucester to slip away, unnoticed.

"It's not that I object to the character in any way; it's just that I have no bond with him, no empathy. I don't believe in Kent as a real being, and there are times I feel he is there simply for the convenience of the plot. To sit in the stocks. To get pushed here and there and even places he can't possibly be in. He's shoved into disguises, given different accents, all as the action requires. I mean, he doesn't have the same intrinsic interest that the other roles have. Edgar is another master of disguises, but his are interesting. Look at poor Tom. I've heard Lear going on about how Kent stands for virtue and loyalty and God knows what. The truth is, Kent's a nonentity." Kent's voice, which has become more heated, calms to meekness once more.

"I'm only telling you this so you know what I have to deal with. What I'm up against. I mean, how can Kent stand beside such roles as Cordelia,

Goneril, Lear himself of course," the voice drops humbly, "even your own role."

The voice pauses, perhaps expecting a reply. None comes. Probably Kent is merely rehearsing what he is going to say. Gloucester digs his fingers into the back of his neck. Headaches are supposed to originate in this area. Right in the hindbrain.

"So I lash out. I don't care what's in front of me or what the consequences might be. I just react. I see one thing and nothing else. I'm confident now that you're not going to forget any lines tonight, are you Gloucester?"

Gloucester turns carefully, using his whole body. His heart is overflowing with good feeling, particularly towards the repentant Kent.

"Know this Kent: tonight is the last night I play Gloucester. You are welcome to the role." He gestures largely. "I detect a common interest here, a convergence of feeling, for I have no great love for my role either, nor for the whole play for that matter. Let us have this understanding then. Just between us. I will stand down and promote you for my role. As to my future role, I'm prepared to take a supportive part until Lear decides on a new play. I'm voting for *A Midsummer Night's Dream*," grandly, "I'm putting myself forward as Bottom."

"That's very kind of you, Gloucester," Kent says carefully. "Let's just run through a few lines now," he gives a hard, dry laugh that wracks his chest like a cough, "just to limber up a little. Pretend you're teaching me your speeches, that you are grooming me for your role, which is actually true." Kent dissimulates, "In fact I'm not at all clear on all of your speeches. How does that one go that begins, *Love cools, friendships fall off, brothers*, um . . ."

"That's easy. *Love cools, friendships fall off,
brothers divide: in cities, mutinies; in countries,
discord; in palaces, treason; and the bond cracked
between father and son*, I mean, *son and father*."

Kent's face breaks into a smile.

"A pretty speech; and well delivered." He takes a deep breath.

"Now let's try something a bit further on," he says encouragingly. "I'm a bit unclear on that scene with Edgar, your loyal son. Can you shoot me the speech that begins, *O you mighty Gods?*"

"That's just about as easy. Let's see:

O you mighty Gods!

This world I do renounce (that's very apt, Kent) *and in your sights*

Shake patiently my great affliction off"

he falters,

"*To quarrel with ...*" flings his arm up.

" *... your great opposeless will,*" Kent supplies, his smile dropping.

" *... opposeless will,* look Edgar, I mean . . ."

"*My snuff and loathed part of nature ...* Come on come on," Kent's voice rising sharply, his eyebrows pulling together.

"*My snuff and loathed part of nature ...* Dear Kent, I can school you at our leisure, right now..."

"*My snuff and loathed part of nature,*" Kent says in a dangerously low voice.

"I have a pain," Gloucester announces.

"*My snuff and loathed part of nature*

Should burn itself out," Kent screams, his face twisted with rage.

Edgar finds himself in the church. A single candle burns on a stool where the altar once stood. Its flickering light sketches cathedral shadows on the walls. I used to know some poetry. Other than Shakespeare. Bits of scripture. It wasn't always like this, the way we see it now, one thing after another, so much tension in the jaw, a yearning for death.

'Look here

the legs are two wheels;

the body is a wagon

full of things.'

Aye, aye. Hold onto the right and true path. It is possible to come to an understanding and hold onto that understanding. Never forget that.

He sits down in one of the pews in the choir and stares at the candle, folding his fingers neatly in front of him. Between his knuckles the candle flame glows but does not burn his flesh. How does the rest of the verse go?

'Five men drive

the wagon

and one is not

like the other.'

That would be the five senses. That by which we apprehend and are reassured. The flame glows inside his flesh but does not burn it. It bends under his gaze. Curan lies curled up inside the flame, a tiny salamander not yet born.

'Where the heart went

I saw the brain

run.'

The candle flame burns. He is standing near Curan and Extra. Neither notice him. They stand with their arms limply by their sides, staring at each other, neither saying a word. Behind them Fleance is lying on a stretcher, his eyes closed.

Hold on to the right and true path. The candle flame passes through his flesh.

He is in the forest. The leaves rattle. He is waiting for death. He can sense the presence of the para-beings. Some are near. Very near. Inside their eyes the salamander burns.

'If space goes naked

with what

shall they clothe it?'

I am being vouchsafed these visions. I hold them in trust. Each is a clue. A piece of jigsaw. When it is finished I will be complete and death will arrive in search of me. When I find it, the answer will be in front of me. Complete in all its details. Something to be grasped in its entirely, all at once.

The candle flame flickers and heels over towards the sound of voices in the main body of the church.

Edgar is standing beside Lear and Cordelia, among the clutter of make-up gear. They are embracing, as they do before every performance. Her expression is of utter vulnerability. She clings to him, unwilling to let him go. Lear's face is uplifting in noble profile.

The voices are insistent and have come nearer.

"No, Edmund. Right now. This skittering second. We need something before the performance. There's no way we can make it otherwise." Cornwall's nasal voice.

"That's right, we won't make it. I can't remember a bloody thing. You'd better give us one, Edmund." Albany's complaining squawk.

"Shut up!" Cornwall's voice again, penetrating and insistent.

Edgar stares at the candle flame.

'If mountains shiver in the cold

with what

will they wrap them?'

The three come into view. Cornwall and Albany are quarreling.

"Shut up yourself," Albany says petulantly. "I'm in this as much as you are."

"Get fucked," Cornwall says thickly.

Albany makes a grab for Cornwall and they both stumble. Cornwall trips over the step of the choir, and curses.

Edmund says grimly, "Oh you'll make it all right. You'll sweat it through." The tin rattles in his palm. "It'll be worth it; there'll be a feast tonight."

Cornwall drops on his knees in front of Edmund and begins fumbling at his belt.

"I'll blow you for one now. Just one. One."

"Yes, Edmund," Albany drops to his knees too.

Cornwall pushes Albany away.

"I told you to get fucked," Cornwall says harshly. "Don't make me have to do it."

Albany begins to cry.

Edmund swings his boot at Cornwall, who dives to avoid it, uttering a sharp, animal cry and reaching desperately for the tin. He connects with it as Edmund's boot connects with his groin, and he goes down with a grunt. A few pills spill on the floor. The Dukes make a wild grab for them as Edmund swings his boot again.

"When the moment comes. Only when the moment comes," he hisses at them, scooping up the pills.

Albany moves his hand slyly up to his mouth.

Edgar is left alone again. The flame glows.

He is standing beside Regan. She is smoothing down her hair with a comb of inlaid mother-of-pearl. Again and again. Her hair parts like water. The same gesture, finger bending back supply. As he watches, the movement slows until the comb is hardly moving.

She turns around and stares at him.

There is nothing to think about. Thought can be abandoned. And all its deserted landmarks. All he need do is hold fast to the true path and await the one who is hunting him, even now, down a curve of dark. No further cerebration is necessary. To see the whole, the complete picture, with all the pieces of the jigsaw in their proper place and relation, thought is no help. It is the nature of thought to deal only in fragments;

perception to apprehend the whole.

Having solved this he can travel, more or less where the spirit takes him, without leaving the church. The flame makes a hole for his eyes, and through those holes he can see the world. *Tom's a cold.*

Now he's with Oswald, who's bending over, spooning food into Little Extra who's grown too listless to want to eat. She is propped up on a pillow and Oswald is crouching in front of her. Her mouth moves mechanically. Oswald's face is haggard, his movements slow and deliberate. Little Extra points to something above them.

"Look!"

Hold on to the right and true path.

'No-one may trace

the footstep on the water.'

He is standing backstage. Edmund is leading Caliban on a leash. He hammers a stake into the ground and ties the ape to it. They are out of sight of the audience. Edmund leans forward and kisses the animal on the nose, lightly. He is whistling.

He is standing beside Regan. She is smoothing down her hair. Her comb is inlaid with mother-of-pearl. Her hair parts like water. The same gesture; fingers bending back. Her hair is a black stream that divides at the knuckles. Is he repeating the previous moment, a brief, backward loop in time, or? Or. Regan turns slowly and stares at him.

The candle flame weaves and shadows. His jaw moves sideways. Curan! Curan! Could I hold you in my arms just once?

He's back in the forest, but something's different this time. The candle is no longer glowing. He's no longer in the church. He's actually out in the forest. This is not a manifestation. He can touch the leaves, smell the moist earth. He's looking back at the camp and the stage. The whole human universe has shrunk to this pitiful circle of light.

How did he get here? Either he has just discovered teleportation or. Or he's suffered a blackout. It's probably Regan, he thinks. She didn't like me hanging around.

Firmly he makes his way back to the church, his business there unfinished. No-one takes any notice of him. Surprising how, despite the fact that his secret is still not known, he has become an outsider, like Oswald. A person others ignore. A person who might as well be invisible.

He enters the church with the eerie feeling he is going to see himself sitting in quiet contemplation in the choir. Of course the choir is empty, he hardly needed to assure himself on that score.

His eye is caught by something gleaming on the floor, half hidden under the steps to the choir. A tiny round white tablet.

One the Dukes must have missed.

Cordelia sets out the jars of make-up in a neat row removing the caps and placing them beside each jar. She uses the paint sparingly, knowing that when it is gone it may never be replaced. Two slim brushes, one broad and one narrow, are placed beside the jars. A jar of water. A dry cloth. How wonderful it would be, she thinks, to have a set of real oils and some canvas. To paint the cast as she sees them, in their characteristic postures. To paint the river and its landscapes, the black, sliding river, the quantum slipperiness of the forest, the tattered villages and deserted towns; to touch this world with paint and hold it there, fast and sure, framed and varnished.

In the meantime she will have to be content with exercising her skill on the faces of the cast, bringing each character alive and volatile; to create with a few brief strokes the genius of the mask.

Even Regan will submit to this from the fingers of Cordelia. She does not even glance at her fair sister but fixed her attention on the mirror as her face takes shape. Her eyebrows are thickened, cheeks made pale; vicious embittered lines appear around her eyes. She gives herself a hard, calculating look.

"Perfect," Cordelia murmurs.

Goneril is next. The oblong of her face becomes sinister, rouged to harlotry; mouth set and cruel. She smiles widely at Cordelia.

The Fool is her favourite mask. She makes him up as a clown with large, surprised rings around his eyes which are themselves droopy and melancholy. Mouth wide and grinning. He does a tap-dance and puts on his floppy dunce's cap with the bell on the end. Laughing, she beckons to him and completes the picture with two spots of colour in each cheek. After she has finished him, he moves off to one side, carefully takes out his upper dentures, wraps them in a rag, and places them in a pocket in his clown's suit. He notices Edgar watching him and grins back, toothless. In Edgar's own voice he says,

"*You are much deceived; in nothing am I changed but in my garments.*"

Edgar turns quickly away.

They are crowding around now, each vying to be next for the touch of the brush. Painting them, Cordelia imagines that she is their creator; that this gaudy procession proceeds from the secret knowledge of her fingers. That she, Cordelia, is the one to give their characters the finishing touches. To take their incompleteness and round them off, ready to be set walking to the stage, the paint new and shiny on their foreheads.

Edmund ambles forward, grinning insolently at Cordelia, holding her eye while she paints him, exaggerating his swaggering leer as she blackens his eyelids and eye sockets. Briskly she roughs in dark lines along his jowls and shakes his cheeks with grey. Keen though he is to engage her, he cannot help a few sidelong glances into the mirror at the emerging Edmund. His chin recedes. Weak, craven lines appear around his mouth.

Coolly she stands back and surveys her handiwork. Has she done enough? Is he complete? He stares at her breasts then looks at the cadaverous visage in the glass.

Thou, Nature, art my goddess; to thy law
My services are bound.

"You have excelled yourself tonight, madam," he says, letting his eye slide down the smooth curve of her neck. *Now gods, stand up for bastards.*

"Let us hope your performance stands to scale," she says evenly, dipping the brushes in water and running them through her fingers.

"Madam, you can rest assured on that count." Edmund replies gravely, his eyes fastened on the mirror.

Oswald finds a spot near the stage and a little to one side. There he sits Little Extra down, wrapped in a blanket against the faint evening chill, and secures a pillow behind her.

Let the heathlings paint their faces! He, Oswald, has no need of it. His face speaks for itself. No-one will mistake him for the hero. His course has long ago been set, the terrible entropy of the Sickness deep at work in his bones. He turns his back to the stage and brings his hands together, palm to palm, his forefingers resting on his lips. Just a little more time, Lord, I will leave the company of madmen; I'll shake the dust of this Shakespeare Company from my heels and find a quiet place. He looks down at Little Extra.

A quiet place.

Edgar passes and gives him a haunted look. Little do you know, Edgar, that your secret is known. Even to one such as Oswald.

Kent stands with his feet apart and his chest thrown out while Cordelia puts on his make-up. His facial lines are uplifted, his hair swept back. He assumes a proud, ferocious expression.

"Do you think," he asks wistfully, "a dwarf could play the role of king?"

"I'm sure," Cordelia replies gently, "That Kent can play any part he chooses."

Kent throws his shoulders back as he has seen Lear do, and thrusts out his chin. He is tall. Taller than a mountain. Every inch a king. He stares down at himself in the mirror. *The same, your servant Kent.* One day to be king!

Under Cordelia's deft brush something of Curan's beauty emerges but the lines are weak, the expression foppish. Here is Curan, all wide-eyes and gossipy; courtier, sycophant, dilettante, pretty-boy. I am a Minor

Role. As she bends over me, ruffling my hair up into the most outrageous courtly fashion, I smell sweet grass; a touch of jasmine. I see her running through a field filled with bright sunlight, her hair jumping in the wind. She is laughing and throwing her arms wide.

It is you I love, Cordelia, as Regan well knows. Even if I lie with her and become her mistress, it is your love that will bear me through.

Cordelia says, almost inaudibly, "Take care, Curan, lest you mistake the nature of the play."

I reply with my most artless look.

Cordelia works on Gloucester longest of all. His square, stolid face is the ultimate challenge for her brushes and paints. With the others, it is a matter of bringing out inherent qualities; with Gloucester, she must transform that confused, dull material into an aging noble. Kind of heart but credulous, blundering. There's something of Gloucester there if only she can find it; reshape the clay of his face.

Gloucester hardly seems to see her. Already he is walking the upward slope that leads to the play. The bulk of it is clear in his mind now. The few grey patches that are left will, he trusts, take form on stage.

It is a peculiar, barren territory, the few minutes before performance. For some reason Kent is there with him, in this empty time, walking the treadmill of his lines, just up ahead or close behind. He needs to throw Kent out of his mind. Surely his grand offer earlier has stopped the bastard's whining. Why shouldn't Kent be Gloucester? Being Gloucester isn't all it's cracked up to be. He made that clear to Kent earlier in the circle. A familiar *déjà vu* surrounds his feelings about Kent. It's a frightening thought. How does change enter a closed universe?

Something is starting to take place in the mirror. As he watches it Gloucester thinks about Kent. He'll probably have to talk to Mainchance about him sooner or later. Lear has a particular reason for keeping the dwarf as Kent; he confessed it one day when they were smoking some of Lear's river weed together, just as they had done in the old days on the river before The Shakespeare Company when the bigger boats still plied the ports. It was simply a question of the stocks, he explained. The stocks are just the right size for the dwarf; and they are a handy size for carrying around. If they change the part they will need to build new stocks. Larger ones. Who would build them? And, anyway, who would want to clutter up the barge with something like that?

"Hold still, what do you find so amusing?"

Gloucester realizes he's been giggling. Cordelia sketches pouches under his eyes, suggesting both age and indulgence. He knows the face that is taking shape in the mirror. He has seen it before. He has cursed it many times. The ponderous old fool: *These late eclipses of the sun and moon portend no good to us.*

So they believe Gloucester is finished, no longer able to hold down a role. He could show them. Give him a good role in some other play. Just try him! What is there to being Gloucester but to suffer humiliation and degradation every night? How long will Kent stick it?

To Cordelia, Gloucester says, "I badly need a massage. It feels as if the whole of my spinal column is seizing up. The tense muscles are putting pressure on my lymph nodes and cutting off the circulation in my arms. It's painful for me to lift my arms above my shoulders."

Briskly she rubs his back, digging her fingers into the muscles on his shoulder and upper arm.

"I'll do it," he says. "For Mainchance."

She stands back and critically surveys her handiwork. Still some missing element. He has not yet come alive.

Gloucester glances at himself in the mirror. An ashen, incomplete face returns his look. Its lips begin to move. It is trying to tell him something. He leans forward the better to lip read. *All dark and comfortless*, the lips say.

He turns to Cordelia.

"You know that opening scene, when the king puts you to that silly test of love?"

Cordelia nods.

"Can't you just tell him what he wants to hear?"

Lear's face barely needs changing. Its lines seem to flow with the brush; a faint accentuating of the eyebrows, the beard thickened and silvered. The sweaty shine taken off his face.

Already he is Lear. You can keep your moody Hamlet and magicked Macbeth; for febrile Moor and your macho Coriolanus. Lear! Now that's an actor's role!

Cordelia leans over and kisses his forehead.

Her own face she does lasts of all, hurriedly, in the mirror. A light red to the lips. Exaggerate the firm strength of the mouth. One stream of hair down across the breast as Ophelia used to wear it. Lighten the eyelids and sockets. As she works she wonders, vaguely, where Edgar is. She has to paint him twice; once for Edgar in the opening scenes and then for Poor Tom.

Never does she leave herself enough time.

The audience has grown. There are twenty, perhaps thirty not counting the children and emaciated dogs. They huddle under blankets, although it is not cold, and stare mesmerized at the stage lanterns, glowing like two soft yellow suns on either side of the stage. It is the lanterns that draw them more than anything. Their faces are bloodless, as if shaded grey by Cordelia's brushes.

Watching them, Lear takes a moment to reflect on his earlier fear of them, his sense that they were reanimated bodies, occupied by spirits fearful of the afterlife. Equally, they could be bodies that have simply kept on walking around after their spirits have fled. Deserted them for some better place. Both notions, seeming opposites, reduced to the same conclusion. Bodies that have forgotten to lie down.

It is always a mistake to consider the audience too deeply just before a performance. Despite words that thunder in the black book, Babylon is just another place, another audience. Another meal. It wouldn't matter if they played to the walking dead. Why worry? Let the dead bury the dead, it said in the black book. That is very practical advice. It is happening right here, in this little town. Corpses bury corpses and lie down in the same grave.

Lear turns to one of the Lords of Babylon; he gestures to the city, the theatre, and the halls.

"We all died in the holocaust. All this is a fading dream. It does not have a continual existence, or true substance as the world knows."

He finds himself straying behind the old church and into the graveyard to have a quiet moment with himself. To sit and breathe deeply before the performance begins. The huddle of dull-eyed people waiting for the play to start floats into his mind.

I am no different from those ones, he realizes. I am just like them. I take the role of Lear. I draw life from it. Sustenance. It is my conduit to the world. Yet every morning I awaken in the palace of Death. What did they call it? Dis. The Palace of Dis. I feel the marble flagstones beneath my feet, the sunlight hurting my eyes.

I will live in the Crystal Theatre forever.

Edmund passes among the audience, laughing and jovial, holding out his hat. He is frantically cheerful, face locked in a ferocious grin.

"Roll up, roll up!" he shouts into the darkness. "Roll up for the greatest show on Earth. The Shakespeare Company plays Babylon tonight! Admittance by contribution."

His face shines in the lantern light.

"Any boys and girls who want to meet Caliban the famous and friendly ape, can do so after the show. If you bring something special along with you. Roll up, roll up! The Shakespeare Company plays Babylon tonight!"

From the shadow beside the stage, Lear gestures him away. Does the Fool still think he works in the circus?

The Fool comes up and stands beside Lear. He gestures to Edmund.

... and pat, he comes, like the catastrophe of the old comedy: my cue is villainous melancholy, with a sigh like Tom o' Bedlam.

Edmund mimics Lear's gestures back to him, grinning at the audience. Some children look up at him curiously. One of them, a girl with tawny hair, speaks low to another. Edmund bends over them and opens his shirt.

"*Is there any cause in nature that makes these hard hearts?*" The Fool asks Lear.

From where I'm positioned, behind the back curtain of the stage ready to serve as prompt for the opening crowded scenes, I can see the audience through a convenient rip in the curtain. The group Edmund has been talking to draw my attention; particularly a girl a little younger than me and a boy perhaps Fleance's age. The girl is staring at the stage with rapt attention and barely suppressed excitement.

Extra comes over and stands beside me. She's going to be one of Lear's retinue in the first scene. I gesture through the rip in the curtain for her to look at the pair I've noticed. She glances listlessly through the curtain and turns away. Curan and Extra are no longer friends. Extra's been moody and difficult since I refused to hug her earlier, after I had returned from the forest.

Most of the cast are assembled behind the curtain. The moment has arrived. Where's Edgar? We need more bit players, the crowd scenes are awfully thin. I try to catch Extra's eye but she won't look at me. I want to make amends and be friends again. Here's some last minute touches to the make-up. How many people have gathered out there? Thirty? Forty? Was that the whole village? Did Edmund get anything from the hat?

Lear adjusts his brooch, pulls at the crotch of his breeches. Where's my crown? It's made of real pewter. He lifts his profile.

Putting on a simple cloak that covers his royal garb and affords some element of disguise, Lear walks out on stage and stares around at the audience. One by one the faces swing towards him.

He bows low.

"Ladies and gentlemen of Babylon, we play for you tonight a timeless and ancient drama. The story itself, I believe, goes back to the very origins of our culture. The props, as you can see, are archly post-modern; the play, the unabashed text; the cast, all professionals.

"Ladies and gentlemen, we, The Shakespeare Company, present, *The Tragedy of King Lear!*"

I hit a gong which makes a large, mellow sound. Lear vanishes off stage and Kent and Edmund enter, Gloucester between them.

"*I thought the king had more affected the Duke of Albany than Cornwall.*" Kent, in a ringing voice.

"*It did always seem so to us,*" replies Gloucester, at the beginning of that same circle.

The play has begun.

Sitting in the lotus pose in the gloom of the church, Edgar meditates. Sitting like this he feels rooted through his spine to the earth. At least it is some assurance against suddenly being transported physically to some other location.

He has set himself a primary question: What is the nature of body? For if roles like Edgar and poor Tom could be set aside, the body was not so easily dealt with. It is an urgent question now that he can feel the tendrils of the Sickness eating deeply into his flesh. The world, in a swell of waves, is beating on his face. What is his body but guts and blood? Isn't it one and the same as the role he plays; Edgar, poor Tom or whoever? It is easy to leave his role behind. To forget it. To have no name. And to have no name is to have no body; for the word is flesh. Is that how it goes?

A body can be left behind, as a role is, surely. Not to come home to, as he had done earlier with the aid of a candle; or to take with him, as when he materialized in the forest; but to be left behind completely.

Why is this denied him? Hasn't he sought death with the fervour of a lover, hounded by the hellish smile of Curan? How does Oswald cope, having the Sickness and walking among the living? He seems to have come to an understanding, still inhabiting his stricken body but with an amused detachment, an equanimity Edgar can only envy. When the moment finally comes, and the moment can't be far off, when Oswald has to die, he will simply lie down, that knowing smile still hovering an inch above his lips.

But Edgar is not content to wait out his time, as Oswald is doing; Oswald does not have to deal with a hopeless, torturing love, disgusting the flesh with its joy. It is all very well for him to be detached and cynical. He is lucky. How can one be detached and cynical, and at the same time burning up with love? Oswald's way cannot be Edgar's.

Bending his mind down through his emotional centres, Edgar attempts to destroy his love for Curan. To burn it out of him. If that can be destroyed, the body will follow soon after. If that can be destroyed he will, like Oswald, become a Cheshire smile, a cipher. Then he will be free to leave his body along with his roles; he will no longer need to grind his teeth or scrabble on the floor for Edmund's pills.

He will not need to call upon a succubus with a courtier's smile.

It is not so easy to root out love, he discovers. It seems as if his desire is woven into the fabric of his flesh with threads of fire. When he dissolves the image of Curan, attempting to blast it from his mind, it reforms again somewhere else. He sees her lying on the grass bathed in moonlight, pale thighs naked; catches a glimpse of her face, nestled into his shoulder.

He tries another tack. If his love cannot be banished, like Edgar, from the kingdom of his mind, perhaps it can be changed, transformed into compassion or the like; transmuted into some substance that will not burn the body.

As he turns his energies inwards to effect this, he hears Lear's voice shouting from the stage.

"*Peace, Kent!*
Come not between a dragon and his wrath.
I loved her most, and thought to set my rest
On her kind nursery. Hence, avoid my sight!
So be my grave my peace, as here I give
Her father's heart from her."

The play has begun. Lear is revoking his love for Cordelia. Edgar will soon be required on stage to play victim to Edmund's machinations.

He turns back into himself. He is no further. His efforts are fruitless. An enormous despair descends; he can do nothing. He is a plaything of the stars. Let the powers stand forth! Let them be seen!

A tall bird stands in front of him, glowing with a faint luminosity. It is of the same generic type as that adorning Edmund's chest, but jewels are set in the plumage of its head and wings. Rapidly it swivels its head, surveying Edgar with each eye alternately.

"What do you want?" it asks in a harsh voice. "I can show you any landscape you wish to name, any world you please."

The bird looks around with evident distaste.

"You don't have to stay in this place. It's a dreadful hole."

Edgar bows his head before the para-being.

"Will I leave Curan behind?"

The bird lifts one leg and cocks its head in a listening posture, then fixes him with a remorseless eye.

"Unfortunately not. You will fashion her from available materials. For example, if I put you on a deserted island within a week you would have discovered her footprint in the sand. If I put you on top of a mountain you would hear her voice when the wind started shouting in empty spaces. Place you in the desert and you will hear the rustle of her skirt in . . ."

"Then let me die!"

"You will find death," the bird cackles. "All you need to do is to learn how to read the signs. Death is here, all around you; every moment the key is placed in front of you.

"Find your Curan, Edgar. Embrace her once and your wish will come true. Allow her embrace and your blood will turn to dust."

Edgar bows his head.

From where I'm positioned I have a good view of the play as it unfolds, when I'm not on stage that is. The opening scenes go well, in fact The Shakespeare Company has never been in better form. Gloucester makes his way stoutly through the lines, delivering them with a reckless bravado. Goneril loud, overbearing, waspish; Regan silky, mean and brooding. Edmund's lines emerge with a brashness that makes up for his wretched acting. Cordelia is all purity and strength, dazzling in her stage white. Kent struts the stage, shoulders back, drawn up to his full height, making a convincing job of defying Lear in the first scene.

But it is Lear to whom our eyes are drawn. He is the magnet at the centre of the action. From his first entry onto the stage, his first royal speeches, his terrible mistaken anger at Cordelia and Kent, there is a special mark of fate upon him. What I am witnessing is an actor rising to the greatness of his role, lifting the cast with him. Unaccountably, tears begin to roll down my cheeks as he banishes Cordelia from the land, as if I'm just seeing the play for the first time.

My eyes are also drawn back to the pair who are now sitting at the front of the audience. The rest of the faces are just white blobs but these two stand out sharply in focus. The girl is watching the stage with a prurient fascination; her lips parted slightly, her hands folded tensely on her knees. The boy might be her brother; he is handsome and clear-eyed, following the play with ferocious concentration, his eyebrows furrowed and lower lip pushed out. Every so often, in an unconscious gesture, the girl pushes her long tawny hair away from her face.

I'm still watching them as the first scene ends and Lear comes backstage. There is a thin film of sweat on his forehead.

"Have you seen Edgar?" he asks.

I shake my head.

"Get ready to take his role. You can play it, I suppose?"

Edgar. I've never given his role much thought, but I tell Lear I can play it. Funny when I try to bring Edgar into my mind I can't picture him.

Lear thumps the ground with his stick.

"You bastard!" he shouts.

Humbly, Edgar says to the bird, "Let me ask you one thing."

"I shall," the bird replies, "but I'm not obliged to answer. There are strict conventions governing these matters."

"Can you show me death? I mean take me there. Give me a foretaste of what it will be like to be loosed from the body. That is why I am meditating here. To solve the question of the body that I might more easily leave it behind."

The bird nods his head in assent.

"Within the grammatical terms of your enquiry, yes; I am able to perform that particular trick. Whether I may, should or shall is another matter. Again there are certain conventions governing this kind of thing."

"What sort of conventions?"

"For example, you may have to find the right formula for the question.

Or you may have to ask three times in line with time-honoured practice. The most usual convention is that these conventions are not revealed to you at the beginning." It begins preening its feathers, its beak clacking against the jewels in its wing.

Edgar feels power surging through him. Determinedly he bends his will upon the half creature.

The bird spreads its wings. It begins to break up, dissolving into pinpricks of light.

"Yes, you can always use force," its voice continues unctuously. "That is another convention. You get your wish." Only its beak remains, clacking to the rhythm of its words. "Remember though, there is an unpredictability in these matters. Sometimes it matters. There's nothing we can do about that. That's at the heart of all things, the massive level; matter jumps about. You may not expect the result."

Its beak finally vanishes and the last three words boom at Edgar from all around him.

He is no longer in the church.

He is nowhere. Nowhere presses closely around him. There is nothing before or after; before drops back, after leaps ahead. Nothing for the eye to light on, or eye to light. Nothing presses closely around him.

Except. Except one point of light, or minute intrusion, as if the vanishing bird has left some speck of itself behind.

He rises from the lotus position and begins walking, the feel of solid ground beneath his feet. He wonders about this before realizing that the very notions of 'walking' and 'solid ground' are, in the context at least, very much a convention.

As he walks he begins to hear music he immediately identifies as 'Songs My Mother Taught Me' by Anton Dvorak, sung in faultless soprano:

'Now that my own dear children
Learn the songs I teach them

Tears fall from my eyelids
From my eyelids
Sounds of weeping reach them.'

He is struck by incomprehensible anguish. This is not my anguish, he realizes. It is something else. Something left over from a previous lifetime.

He hurries on, leaving the zone of sorrow and sad music behind. The speck of light appears to be growing. At the same time he faces the prospect that it might be shrinking, moving away from him; that it might vanish altogether.

Is this death, chasing around some silly dot of light?

There is a new quality in the nowhere. A frequency, a sound. It is like the grinding of teeth, but enormously magnified. As it passes through him he feels his whole atomic structure vibrate. It is some kind of tsunami, rushing through the fabric of his nothingness. Another like it and he might shake to bits.

He has come to what appears to be a window. All it shows is a meaningless swirl of points of light. He could be looking at galaxies or sunlight breaking up on water. This is replaced by Lear's face.

"You bastard," Lear says.

Edgar hurries on, still following his distant beacon. More windows appear, some with scenes that have no meaning to him, others he recognizes as feverish products of his own imagination. Among these are several of Curan in attitudes of debauchery; sometimes with Edmund, with Regan in a moonlit glade, with Extra. There is one that interests him that does not appear to belong to this category; Curan is lying on the bracken of the forest, clinging onto the root of a tree, her face twisted in effort.

As he glances at these pictures he realizes that they no longer provoke in him the anguish, shame and jealousy they might once have. He is becoming detached from his emotions. Soon these pictures of a wanton

Curan will mean nothing to him at all, like the other pictures. There's one of a man and a woman sitting at a table eating and chatting. Edgar doesn't know these people. They don't arouse any emotional reaction in him. They have the credibility of perfect strangers.

At the same time the anguish and jealousy are still in existence. They have not vanished, but have become free-floating entities. Occasionally, like a moth, something brushes his heart and the old emotion jumps, straining at the rim of dark. At such moments he is swept by a desperate fear: I am losing my love for Curan.

It is drifting away from him. He is walking away from it.

There are no more windows. The nothingness is perfect, but for one blemish. Yet even that nothingness is no more than a skin or membrane. A warp in the weave. There is the pressure of shape and form behind it.

He is walking down an incline. The closer he gets to the light the steeper it becomes. He is in a tunnel, the sides closing in, the plastic fabric of time and space opening out in front. The light is now as large as a distant doorway.

A voice sounds close, almost in his ear. It is Edmund, his bastard brother.

"My father compounded with my mother under the dragon's tail, and my nativity was under Ursa Major; so it follows I am rough and lecherous. 'Sfoot! I should have been that I am had the maidenliest star in the firmament twinkled on my bastardizing. Edgar - "

The mellow light is all around him. He can see Edmund now, strutting up and down declaiming his lines. The slope is steeper; he is being tipped towards the page of light opening out in front of him. Edmund continues, skipping phrases and mangling the sense,

"... and pat he comes, the catastrophe... my cue is... villainous melancholy... O these eclipses do portend... these divisions... "

Edgar is thrust onto the stage. The light he has been following across the trackless wastes of nothing he identifies as the flow of the stage lanterns. Edmund stares at him in amazement. Behind Edmund, Edgar can see Curan about to enter the stage, dressed not in her foppish courtier's livery but as the son of an Earl, as Edgar himself.

Edgar turns to Edmund.

"*How now, brother Edmund! What serious contemplation are you in?*"

Behind stage Lear puts his head in his hands.

Curan enjoys these early, nerve-wracking scenes. The polite veneer, the semblance of civility still holds, despite the air of feverish haste and the partially formed outline, glimpsed here and there, of the monstrous doom to come. The actors too, it strikes Curan, share this reckless haste as the scenes shuffle forward, tripping on and off stage, frantically adjusting costumes; enmeshed in the headlong tumble of events.

Only Cornwall and Albany spoil the general effect by constantly missing their entries and exits and petering out in the middle of lines. Often it's Edmund who prods them into action with a quiet kick or an elbow in the ribs.

I'm helping Cordelia fix Cornwall's costume, which consists of a black nineteenth century smoking jacket with ruffled sleeves, when there's an unscripted scream from the stage:

"Gloucester, haven't you forgotten something!" It is Kent's shrill voice. I race back to my spy hold and job as prompt.

It is the stocks scene and Gloucester has forgotten to stay on stage. He meets Lear at the back curtain. Lear attempts to propel him back on stage. I'm frantically hissing the lines he needs, so loud I'm sure the audience can hear.

"*I'm sorry for thee friend*
'tis the Duke's pleasure."

Still hovering near the back of the stage, Gloucester turns in the direction of my voice.

"Kent's gone mad," he says to Lear.

"*I'm sorry for thee friend,*" Regan says, coming up behind Lear.

"*Pray do not, sir.*" Kent yells from the stage, as if Gloucester has delivered his lines. "*A good man's fortune may grow out at the heels.*"

"The Duke's to blame for this," I hiss to Gloucester. Gloucester looks at me blankly. "*'Twill be* taken ill, I mean *ill taken*." I curse at my slip.

"Who?" says Gloucester. "The Duke? Taken ill?"

"Get the bastard off stage," Lear says brutally, to no-one in particular.

"Yes sir!" says Edmund, leaping to his feet.

Resolutely Kent continues his speech, his voice shaking with rage.

"*Approach thou beacon to this under globe...*"

While he is speaking Edmund appears beside Gloucester.

"Come on, Grandad." He grins his big Edmund grin at the audience, and takes Gloucester by the arm. Gloucester dithers. Edmund eases him towards the back curtain.

"*Fortune goodnight, smile once more; turn thy wheel.*" Kent's voice rises to a caterwaul on the last words.

Gloucester is standing beside me as Kent finishes his speech.

"*The Duke's to blame in this,*" he says mournfully.

"It's the Duke's fault," Regan says to Edmund, who puts his finger in his mouth and makes a popping noise.

Lear, the Fool and Extra (as Gentleman) go out onto the stage for the next scene. Lear ignores Gloucester as he goes past. As she passes me Extra turns her head away. Gloucester and I are matched company.

"It's only that one bit I miss," he says to me. "I never miss anything else except the odd line. A small gap in the circle. I just step over it. I don't even see that it's there."

Fleance is getting ready to play Servant to Cornwall. As he changes he turns his back to me, balancing on one leg to put on oversize breeches. I see the thin outline of his buttocks through the material. If I keep watching him he might fall over.

"One small gap," Gloucester says sadly.

"I think Kent is overdoing it," Regan says to Gloucester. "He's making far too much about such a small gap."

I'm shaking a length of sheet tin to provide thunder for the storm scene when Edmund approaches me, flashing his knowing grin.

"What kind of opportunity?" I look at him coldly.

He points to the bulge in his pants.

"My cock has special magical properties. Among other things it confers immunity from the Sickness."

I shake the tin harder.

"You don't expect me to believe that." Curan may only be a foolish courtier but there are limits to her credulity.

Edmund looks around conspiratorially.

"Let me tell you a secret. Very few people know this, but in the very last days a vaccination was discovered. I should know, I was an experimental subject. So was Caliban. That's where I met him. All that stuff about coming from the circus is a cover."

I stop shaking the tin so Lear can rage at the elements. The play is going well again. Lear is pushing his role to ever greater heights, turning himself into an elemental force as huge as the contending winds and rain.

"Listen," Edmund whispers. "The scientists knew they would never be able to distribute their vaccine so they adapted it in such a way that it would be passed on. After they died. They adapted it so it would be produced by the body's busiest little factory, the testicles. It was a last desperate dream to save mankind." He holds his hand up to his forehead. "Alas, they died, even as we recovered."

A terrible moment in the play has arrived. The moment at which Lear begins to crumble under the emotional pressure, saying to himself in a strange, cracked whisper:

"... *My wits begin to turn*
Come on, my boy, how dost my boy, art cold?
I am cold myself..."

Although I have witnessed this scene many times, I feel a shiver up my spine. There is an ancient, cracked quality in his voice I have never heard before. For a dreadful moment I believe that Lear, not Shakespeare's but our own, has gone mad.

Curan's eyes are glued to the spyhole. The boy and girl, with a few others, have moved closer to the stage. She is hugging her knees, staring at the stage, eyes preternaturally wide. The boy is covering his eyes with his hands. The few that have joined them have their eyes fixed rigidly on the stage.

I understand that Lear is right, right to be putting on the play in a place like this. Even if only these two alone followed it and were blinded, however briefly, by its vision, the whole effort would have been worth it.

Edmund is whispering into Curan's ear so close she can feel the warmth of his breath and smell his sharp, male odour; the faint, fishy smell of stale semen spiced with an echo of Caliban. I wish he'd go away. I want to be able to concentrate on my spyhole. I want to be able to watch the girl in the audience; to watch her with the same hopeless fascination with which she is watching the stage. Lear continues:

"*The art of our necessities is strange,*
that can make vile things precious."

It is the same weird, broken voice I heard earlier. This is not Lear's voice.

"Do you understand, pretty one? I had the Sickness and recovered. No-one else in the whole world has done that. Except Caliban and me."

The Fool has danced to the front of the stage. He turns his clown's face this way and that as if looking for something above and beyond the audience, cupping his hand behind his ear in a large gesture. Then he sings in a high, childlike voice directly to the boy and girl at the front,

"*He that has a tiny little wit,*
With a hey, ho, the wind and the rain,
Must make content with his fortune's fit
Though the rain it raineth every day."

"You don't believe me, do you? That I was an experimental subject. There were hundreds of us in cages. Prisoners. Criminals. Criminals with the Sickness, what's more. It was a huge underground lab sealed off from the open air. They took us in there at night in army trucks. Our first job was to load the latest crop of corpses onto the trucks." He looks intensely into the middle distance.

"We were put in cages, like animals. In fact there were animals there too. Caliban was one. There were dogs, chimps, monkeys, you name it. We men and women used to scream at night, just like the animals. They were working down the row I was in, trying different batches of serum. Often the serum killed the subject outright. Mostly it never made any difference. Everybody was dying anyway. I heard them talking when they went into the cages. About this serum that would reproduce itself and transmit itself, just like the Sickness does. When they came into my cage they were saying that the Sickness might have been cooked in some war lab somewhere." His eyes go unfocused in the effort to remember. "I can still remember the code number for the serum. XP3-Q5W. Three days in a row, they shot me up. They talked in front of me as if I wasn't even there. As if I couldn't understand plain language. I must've taken a dozen jabs. They talked about the reaction of an ape who was being given the same stuff, and that the serum was showing signs of taking. Then they started dying. Scientists, doctors, attendants, guards; the whole cast. The trucks stopped bringing replacements. Within four days the whole place was a tomb except for me and one other. I couldn't see him but I could hear him, clanging the bars of his cage. We both nearly starved to death, there in the cages, until the electricity failed and the doors just fell open. Caliban and I escaped."

He gives me a big Edmund grin.

"I walked out of that place carrying a cure. Every baby born from my sperm carries an altered genetic code that makes it immune. It's all in the chromosomes." He taps his crotch and lifts his eyebrows. "Every baby is another chance. Like Goneril's."

"Goneril? Does she believe this?"

He nods sincerely.

"She wants a lot of healthy daughters so she can dream about going to bed with them or watching them from behind the arras."

"And Goneril's baby . . ." I can't bring myself to say it.

He nods.

Lear shuffles out to the front of the stage and joins the Fool. His left side drags heavily.

"*True my good boy. Come, bring us to this hovel.*
Poor fool and knave."

I rattle the tin as hard as I can. Regan and Goneril make high eerie wind sounds.

"*This is a brave night to cool a courtesan,*" the Fool says.

I become aware that there is somebody watching Edmund and me. It is Edgar, standing to one side and behind. He is staring at Edmund with a peculiar fixity. For a moment his eyes alight on me, a glance bright and diamond hard.

"*I'll make this prophecy ere I go.*" The Fool dances on one foot.

"You'll make a bed for me," Edmund says softly. I put my eye back to the spyhole, ignoring Edmund. Lear and Kent have come backstage. The Fool is alone on stage juggling balls and singing, dancing at the same time a sure-footed jig. The boy at the front is looking up at him with open mouthed wonder. Suddenly I feel the girl's eyes probing the back curtain. It seems as though our eyes meet, although she can't possibly see me. Step on a crack you marry a rat.

"Save some for me," Edmund says in the same soft voice.

The Fool is finishing his song as I turn to answer Edmund. Edmund is gone. Already he is walking on stage, whistling cheerfully. Gloucester is there to meet him.

"Alack. Alack! Edmund. I like not this unnatural dealing. When I desired *their leave that I might pity him, they took me from the use of mine*, of mine..."

"*... own house,*" Curan whispers.

"That's right," Gloucester continues in a jerky, mechanical voice, "*... charged me on the pain of their perpetual displeasure, neither to speak of him, entreat for him, nor any way sustain him.*"

Edmund wanders to the front of the stage and looks at the boy and girl.

"*Most savage and unnatural!*"

He is grinning his big, stupid Edmund grin.

The girl's eyes bite at the back curtain.

I feel that Edgar is standing right near me, where Edmund stood. The back of my neck prickles. But when I turn around he's not there. He is busy with Cordelia, changing from Edgar into Poor Tom. Black rings around his eyes give him a wild, staring look. His hair is teased out so that it stands on end. A crown of twigs and plaited vine goes on top of that. He's wearing nothing but some tattered sacking around his waist; his chest and legs are covered in scratches and mud. He turns and looks at me, hissing:

"*Away! the foul fiend follows me!*

Through the sharp hawthorn blow the winds."

Lear wanders over and joins Curan by the spyhole. This meeting between Edmund and Gloucester gives him a brief respite before the harrowing hovel scene and the mock trial at the farmhouse. After that comes the most trying section of the whole play, the plucking out of Gloucester's eyes. Clearly it's Gloucester he's now thinking about as he peers through the spyhole.

Gloucester is making heavy weather of the long 'letter' speech in which he unwisely divulges the content of the letter to Edmund, who will shortly betray him with it.

"Faster," Lear hisses from behind the curtain, "Faster, faster."

"*If he asks me I am ill and gone to bed,*" Gloucester squawks. "*If I die for it, as no less is threatened me, the king, my old master, must,* the king, my master . . ."

Lear rolls his eyes at Curan.

Before he can be prompted, Edmund butts in with the last lines of the scene. Gloucester is supposed to have left the stage but Edmund has given him no time.

"*That which my father loses; no less than all:*
The younger rises when the old doth fall."

This last line he treats as some secret communication between himself and the two avid children.

Kent's already strutting out onto the stage, followed by the Fool and Lear. They pass Edmund and Gloucester going the other way. While Edmund heads towards Curan, kicking aside the Dukes who are lying, apparently extinguished, on the ground, Gloucester heads towards Cordelia.

"What a lot of coming and going there is in this play," he tells Cordelia. In and out. Roundabout. It's enough to make him dizzy.

"It's enough to make me dizzy," he says, glancing at Regan who's sitting nearby on her own, brooding down at her hands.

"Are you content to stay like this forever and ever?" he asks Cordelia. "I mean, in your role. Do you want to remain being Cordelia?" His tongue is thick in his mouth and he's finding it hard to get the form of the question right, as if this were script and he had to remember lines. What he wants to say is that there was a time when he was not Gloucester. He was Polonius, a muddle-headed noble, and before that he was a gambler on the river with Mainchance, plying the boats. He had another name then. Slink. Slink 'n' Mainchance, the terror of the river. They lived well on the suckers and the desperate. And there was a time he was Bottom, that has to be fitted in somewhere. And some minor roles.

Cordelia looks wistful. Absently she touches her lips to the back of her hand.

"I don't mind Cordelia, but there's barely a hundred lines in the whole part. It's really a minor role. I do more work backstage. I'd like to do Juliet. Perhaps Miranda. I wouldn't fit as a Goneril or Regan; I'm not that good an actor."

Gloucester nods, gratified at the direction the conversation is heading. Regan glances up sharply in the direction of Cordelia.

"You're right," she says sweetly, "Curan gets to see more of the action than you do."

"What I want to know is, why do we do it?" Gloucester says stubbornly. "I've come to this understanding quite recently. I'm not sure that it is part of the cycle; but if it's not, it's a sign that the cycle can be broken."

"What do you mean?" Cordelia.

"I mean my understanding is new. Everything else that happens to me has happened before, many times."

"What understanding?"

"That I don't have to keep doing this. They all think I'm losing my marbles. Slink would cut your throat for something like that. I don't have to hang in here."

All three are silent. From the stage Lear's voice comes, already light with madness.

"*When the mind's free*
The body's delicate; the tempest in my mind
Doth from my senses take all else
Save what beats there."

"We do it for him," Cordelia says simply, "Because he's a great actor."

Gloucester nods. It's true. Who would have guessed that Mainchance the gambler would turn out to be a great Shakespearean actor? Who would have put their money on something like that? Sidekick Slink hasn't done so well.

"He's a great actor and this is his greatest role. In this role he can scale the full heights of being," Cordelia goes on, staring dreamily as she does sometimes on the *Earl of Southampton*, gazing at the water and the far shore. "We know we can't scale those heights, no matter what role we were given. It just isn't given to us to know these things. So we do it for him."

"For Mainchance," Gloucester nods grimly in assent. That must be it.

Onstage, Edgar finds his cue without need of prompting, "*Away, away. The foul fiend follows me.*"

Since his dramatic entrance at the beginning of the play, Edgar has not missed a beat, playing his role with a calculated fury that gives the somewhat bland character of the legitimate son a certain ambience. Lear is pleased. Edgar is entirely at one with his role. He circles around Lear, gesturing at him and stabbing with his words.

"*Do poor Tom some charity, whom the foul fiend vexes. There I could have him now, and there,*" he makes grabbing motions with his fists, half punching, half tearing at the air, "*And there again, and there.*"

"Caliban and I walked for three days before finding any human life. The Sickness was completely gone from us. White patches gone. My head had cleared and I could think again. My thoughts were different too, sharp and clear. How the skin feels in Winter. Finally in a small town I found a group of survivors. There was only one woman among them, and she was far gone with the Sickness. Despite that I wanted her. I had to have her." He begins stroking Curan's arm. "The life force was beginning to work in me; the desire was intolerable. Before that I'd never gone for women. Kept company with such as the Dukes. I thought it was a great irony, the only man in the world carrying immunity being gay. An irony

151

like that would have kept me laughing for many years. But when I left that lab a new hunger was born in me." Edmund bows his head humbly.

"Some mysterious force was working miracles in me."

Curan pushes past him to go to Gloucester, carefully skirting his thrust out hips. I want to make sure that Gloucester doesn't miss his next cue.

"*Is no man no more than this? Consider him well,*" Lear's voice from the stage. Another few lines and Gloucester is due on. He's standing moodily by the gap in the curtain we use for entries and exits.

"I go on stage to save Lear," Gloucester says to Curan. "I give him comfort and shelter, a place to work through his madness. A few lines further on and I pack him off to the protection of Cordelia."

"That's right, Gloucester." I nod encouragingly as I have seen Lear do.

"I pay dearly for that act of kindness. What kind of justice is there in that?"

" *... unaccommodated man is no more but such a poor, bare, forked animal as thou art. Off, off you lendings! Come; unbutton.*" Lear starts ripping at his clothes.

I give Gloucester a gentle push in the direction of the stage making sure he has his 'torch', in this case a small oil lamp.

"I'm going to hand in my notice," he says to me as he goes.

"*Here comes a walking fire,*" says the Fool.

"One night I went into the room where she was sleeping and took her. I didn't even care that there were other men in the room. She died in childbirth, she was too far gone with the Sickness, but the child was whole. Small, sturdy limbs. Tiny fists. The inheritors. My children will inherit the world."

The lanterns have been dimmed for this scene, and Gloucester finds himself on a field of reduced horizons. Near the front of the stage, to the left, the Fool is struggling with the mad king. Two swirling shadows coming towards turn into poor Tom and Kent. Poor Tom grabs him by the arm and spins him around, singing,

"*Swithold footed thrice the old;*
He met the night-mare, and her nine-fold
Bid her alight
And her troth plight
And aroint thee, witch aroint thee!"

Gloucester struggles with him. He can hear the king moaning and wailing.

"*How fares your grace?*" Kent says in a dry, contemptuous voice.

It seems to Gloucester that the stage is peopled with figures and shadows. Looking across at the king and trying to make him out there seems to be more than just the Fool with him. Lear is surrounded by cavorting, mocking figures.

"*What are you there?*" Gloucester shouts. "*What are your names?*"

Edmund approaches Cordelia.

"Madam," he says with an exaggerated simper, "I need a little touching up with your magic brushes. Here," pulls open his shirt far enough to reveal the bird's head, "and here."

Fleance takes over as prompt and I go over to Cordelia to be made up as a servant to Cornwall for the eye-plucking scene. Both Extra and I are on stage for this scene and we share the roles of First and Second Servant. First Servant gets to stab Cornwall.

As Extra and I converge on Cordelia, Edmund rouses the Dukes. He takes out his tin box and rattles it in their ears. The Dukes have their hands in each other's pockets.

It's Extra's turn first. She gets a beard and bare, blackened arms. We love dressing up as men and sometimes stick hankies down our fronts to make bulges in our breeches.

Extra looks handsome dressed up as a man with her beard and broadened shoulders. When Cordelia turns away to clean her brushes, I take Extra's hand and give it a gentle squeeze, trying to revive our old intimacy. For a second she allows me to fondle her hand, then shoots me a hateful look and squeezes my little finger hard with her fingernail.

"Ouch!" I whine, as loudly as I can.

Goneril appears backstage with her lute.

"Tonight I will sing," she contrives to whisper grandiosely.

Lear, Kent and Edgar troop off stage as Edmund drags Cornwall on for the brief scene in which Edmund betrays his father to the Duke. As soon as he sees the lute, Lear's face darkens.

"Tonight, Goneril? You must sing tonight?"

"Tonight," she replies, flourishing the lute, "I will sing a seventeenth century pastoral by Thomas Campion. Not 'There Is A Garden In Her Face,' the one I did last time, but . . ."

"Tonight? You must, tonight?"

"You've already delivered that line."

" 'There Is A Garden In Her Face' was hardly suitable for the context.

"This one departure from your 'unabashed text' you have already allowed," Goneril says lugubriously, tuning her lute from which soft, plaintive sounds emerge. "It's an interlude. The audience can have a little munch. I'm sure playscripts in Shakespeare's day were flexible structures. I bet they stopped for the occasional song.

"You'll love tonight's piece, Lear, you really will. It's 'My Sweetest Lesbia' written in 1601, with words adapted from Catullus, the Roman poet."

"It's a matter of dramatic pace," Lear explains patiently. "The momentum. Stop to sing a song and you lose it." He throws his hands into the air despairingly.

Goneril gives all the appearance of having to deal with a difficult, persistent child. "You're making excuses. The song is an ideal lull before the storm. The horrible barbarities of the following acts," her eyes rest dispassionately on Gloucester. "It's a moment's sweet pathos, good king. Your Shakespeare was good at that kind of thing. I'm sure he would have put a song in it at this point himself. If he hadn't been in such a fucking hurry." She makes a grandiloquent gesture.

Edmund has already returned, half carrying Cornwall. Kent, Edgar and the Fool are heading back onto the stage. Lear follows with a dismissive gesture to Goneril who finds the first chord of the song.

" 'My Sweetest Lesbia, let us lie and love,' " she croons. Regan joins her on the second line:

" 'And though the sager sort our deeds reprove

Let us not weigh them.' "

I'm back at the spyhole. Edmund goes past.

"The new human race will be my children," he says, giving me a knowing look, "all of them."

I send Fleance off to be made up as Third Servant to Cornwall. As soon as I look out the spyhole the girl's eyes swivel towards me.

"You can play First Servant," Extra says to Curan. Curan turns away from the spyhole and Extra assumes a martyred expression.

"Why don't you do it?" Curan asks, "I don't mind." Her voice is pitched to a precise indifference.

"Are you going to sleep with Regan from now?" Extra asks in a small voice, not looking up.

"I might even do that," Curan says carelessly, brushing back her hair. "That's certainly a possibility."

They stand with their arms limply by their sides, staring at each other. Extra walks away. "You can do First Servant," she mumbles.

" 'Heaven's great lamps do dive

Into their west

And straight again revive

But as soon as once set is our little light

Then must we sleep one ever during night

Ever during night.' "

Goneril croons softly.

Kent, Gloucester and the Fool troop off stage in Lear's train. Edgar is still on stage delivering a short speech, bidding farewell to his disguise, poor Tom:

"*Who alone suffers, suffers most i' the mind,*

Leaving free things and happy shows behind."

Backstage, Lear is talking urgently to Gloucester.

"This next scene, hateful as it is to you Gloucester, is the climax of the sub-plot and the fruition of Edmund's plotting against his father. In this scene the power of the conspirators reaches a climax."

Over in the make-up area Regan is preparing, slipping up her sleeve an old toothpaste tube full of a red mixture made up by Cordelia. When the time arrives to pluck out Gloucester's eyes Regan will move forward, flash out one hand towards his face while the other, out of sight of the audience, will squirt paint at him. I think it is having paint squirted on his face that really disturbs Gloucester. In that moment he must shut his eyes and experience the terror and blindness of Shakespeare's Gloucester.

Lute in hand, Goneril heads for the stage.

"Do you remember the last scene of *A Midsummer Night's Dream?* There's a wonderful, massive wedding. Everyone gets married to the right partner," Gloucester sighs. "It's a splendid scene, Mainchance. The brides in their sumptuous costumes. The men all smiling and jovial." He seizes Lear's arm.

"That's the play for Babylon."
Goneril is singing the second verse of the Campion song.
" 'If all would lead their lives in love like me
Then bloody swords and armour should not be
No drum or trumpet peacefully sleeps should move
Unless alarms come from the camps of love
But fools do live and waste their little light
And seek with pain their ever during night
Ever during night.'"
Edmund leans over Curan's shoulder.

"Hark! Look at the angel. O she is light." Gesturing in the direction of Cordelia who's standing near the curtain, her head on one side, staring dreamily at the ground, her body rocking faintly to the rhythm of the song.

"She's hot tonight," Edmund whispers hoarsely, his breath swelling in his chest. "She's building up for it. The cycle; I can smell it: ovulation," breathing deeply through his nose, he mouths the word as if swallowing an oyster.

All movement has ceased as Goneril continues the song. Looking at Cordelia, I feel the lifting of the weight of time from my body. The relentless engine of the play has been suspended and we are free-floating, disengaged. Cordelia does not belong to time at all, I realize.

Lear is looking around him, blinking, as if he's only just realized where he is.

Into the silence Goneril's brassy, sonorous voice:
" 'When timely death my life and fortune ends
Let not my hearse be vexed with mourning friends
But let all lovers rich in triumph come
And with sweet pastimes grace my happy tomb
And Lesbia, close thou up my little light
And crown my love with ever during night

Ever during night.'"

"*Twelfth Night* is also very rich in song," Gloucester says to Lear.

Regan, Cornwall, Edmund and Servants (that's Extra, Fleance and me) file out onto the stage to join Goneril. As First Servant I'll be sent off stage almost immediately in search of the traitor, Gloucester. Extra and Fleance will follow a little later.

"*The army from France has landed*," Cornwall says after a kick from Edmund. "*Seek out the traitor Gloucester.*"

"*Hang him instantly*," Regan says.

"*Pluck out his eyes*," Goneril echoes.

I go off stage and find Lear talking sternly to Gloucester.

"Listen, old friend. The wrongs done to you, the atrocities committed on your person in this scene are later revenged. Kent, Edgar, the forces of France, the virtue of Cordelia, serve to right the moral balance of the world. Consider the Universe: it's a balanced proposition, the right proportion of the vertical and the horizontal, the infinite and the attainable; the proper proportion of matter and mind. The Universe, Gloucester, invites itself to a free lunch. We all partake of the feast. It is only our pitiful human vision that would circumscribe it thus," he draws a circle in the air, "and thus," draws another circle, smaller than the first, "with our cold equations.

"So too with the play, which walks the precise line. Order is restored. Without the balance tragedy has no context; in fact tragedy as such is not possible."

"But Mainchance," Gloucester moans, "we have not kept *our* balance. Order has not been restored. We are falling. There is nothing underneath us. We are falling through space at a frightful speed. Can't you feel it?"

Lear stares at him. What can he say? That yes, he too can feel it? And in that falling some parts are moving faster than others. Bits of the world breaking up; meteorites and distant worlds flinging themselves at frightful speeds away from one another: 'And he cried in a mighty voice saying, Fallen, fallen is Babylon the Great, and is become the habitation of devils, and a hold of every unclean spirit.'

He can't say anything like that to Gloucester.

Gloucester turns to Curan.

"You have come for me, have you, dark angel?" Morosely he wanders over to the mirror. There is no reflection. He can see only the dark of the curtain and some make-up jars. He peers closer. There's a small grey spot at the centre. It expands and fills out the whole mirror. The curtain and the make-up jars vanish. Nothing. *Nothing can come of nothing.* The mirror is depthless. Wait, there is something there. The outline of a hood. A cowled figure with a hidden face.

"You have to see this in perspective," Lear says from behind him. "Shakespeare's characters pay a terrible price for their understandings; it's a question of gaining self-knowledge."

To the empty mirror Gloucester says, "My body is on fire. My spine is. Stiff. This poetry is not a cure for headaches." In a moment Extra and Fleance, Servants to Cornwall, will come backstage to help fetch him. First Servant to Cornwall hovers by his side. He will be taken out onto the stage and tied to a chair. His beard will be pulled and insults heaped upon him.

"I have seen a vision," he says to Lear, "of my own death. The pallbearers have come. They never leave without a body. That's customary."

Fleance and Extra appear and take up position on each side of Gloucester. I move in behind him. He tries to say one more thing to Lear but at the last moment the words are gone. His lips open and shut soundlessly. As he passes onto the stage the Fool thrusts his head in front of him.

"*Now a little fire in a wide field were like an old lecher's heart; a small spark, all the rest on's body cold.*"

Lear smiles at me. "It's an amazing thing, Curan, this dedication to one's craft."

Gloucester faces the hard light of the stage, eyes blinking. The chair sits in the middle of the stage. As soon as he sees it he knows he has seen it before, many times. Cornwall and Regan are standing by the chair watching him enter. Gloucester tries to get them in focus. Edmund and Goneril stand silent at the back of the stage. According to the play, they are not on stage during this scene, but Lear has good reasons for allowing them to stay, not least Edmund's ability to keep Cornwall going. Cornwall is sweating hard. This is his last and most demanding scene.

"*Bind fast his corky arms,*" Cornwall says. Regan gives him a cruel smile.

Gloucester finds his lines and stumbles through them thickly.

"*What mean your Graces? My good friends, consider
You are my guests: do me no foul play, friends.*"

Regan steps forward. "*Bind him I say,*" she says sharply to Extra and me, taking Cornwall's line and command of the scene. Cornwall is staring vacantly at Edmund.

As we bind Gloucester I can feel the eyes of the girl in the audience upon me. I plan to turn soon and give her a bold look.

"*Hard, hard,*" Regan screams at us, back to her own lines. It is hard not to obey her. There is a small touch of crimson in each of her cheekbones. We've hardly finished going through the motions of binding him when she leans forward and pulls at his beard. I feel Gloucester jerk back and for a second forget that his beard is false. We can hear Lear behind the curtain, playing prompt for Gloucester.

"*I am your host,*" Gloucester says wildly, starting in the middle of his next speech. His beard is hanging half off.

"*To this chair bind him,*" Cornwall shouts belatedly.

Regan is now standing right over Gloucester. It's frightening, the way she gains ascendancy and power in this scene, shouldering aside the incompetent Cornwall to dominate the scene. There is a beauty in her ferocious unpredictability, her wanton cruelty. I don't want to see that beauty. I'm standing so close to her I can feel the heat coming off her body and her sharp, animal smell.

"*What confederacy have you with the traitors
Late footed in the kingdom?*" Cornwall blurts, veins standing out on his forehead.

"*Be simple answered, for we know the truth,*" snarls Regan, back-tracking to lines Cornwall has skipped. Cornwall looks at her in confusion. Lear hisses something from behind the curtain. Gloucester looks at Regan and Cornwall helplessly. I take a sly look at the girl in the front; her eyes are still fixed on me.

"*To whose hands have you sent the lunatic king?*" Regan goes on, skipping forward again, glaring at Cornwall.

"*And what confederacy have you with the traitors* ..." Cornwall looks appealingly at Edmund. Lear's voice is heard behind the curtain, low and clear like the ghost in Hamlet,

"*I have a letter guessingly set down, which came from
one that's of neutral heart.*"

Gloucester clears his throat.

"*I have a letter,*" he and Cornwall begin simultaneously. Behind the stage, Lear puts his head in his hands.

Gloucester turns to Curan. "Untie me," he hisses.

Regan is watching Gloucester as a ferret watches its prey, her fingers beginning to flex themselves as she makes sure her tube of paint is accessible.

"*Cunning,*" she says, taking Cornwall's line.

"*And false,*" pipes Cornwall, taking her line and apparently finding his place in the text again as he continues,

"*Where hast thou sent the king?*"

"*Dover,*" Gloucester answers in a choked voice.

"*Wherefore to Dover?*" Regan whips back, not giving Cornwall a chance to the line for himself. "*Let him answer that.*"

Gloucester runs his tongue over his lips. Actually it is a very good question, he thinks. If he hadn't sent Lear to Dover none of this might have happened. He might have lived to a happy old age, his beard restored.

"*Let him answer that,*" Regan repeats, trying to prompt Gloucester. Would the old fart never get on with it?

"*I am tied to the stake, and must stand the course,*" Lear's voice comes from behind the curtain. Gloucester shakes his head. What do they want of him? What, in the final analysis, does anyone want of him? If he knew he would bend over backwards to satisfy them. Why does this woman want to torture him? Is it because he loves the old king?

"I must. No. *I am tied to this stake and I must,* yes, *stand the course.*" *Stand the course,* he murmurs to himself, feeling the shape of each word in his mouth. His big speech is coming up. His final act of defiance. What are the opening lines?

He looks up at Regan. She is staring at him with hard, empty eyes, close enough for him to see his reflection in her pupils.

"*Wherefore to Dover?*" she asks in a chilled voice, slow and horribly calm. Before Lear can prompt she mouths his next lines for him. The opening lines of his last grand speech:

"*Because I would not see thy cruel nails.*"

Her fingers begin to creep up to Gloucester's face.

"*Because I would not see thy cruel nails.*"

Gloucester repeats hollowly…

"… *Pluck out his poor old eyes.*"

"*Pluck out,*" Gloucester swallows, "*his poor old eyes.*"

"*Nor thy fierce sister,*" Lear says from behind the curtains.

"… *in his anointed flesh stick boarish fangs,*" Gloucester completes.

Regan's fingers sit either side of his jaw. He can see the red fingernail polish and the flat, dark hair on her wrists.

"*The sea with such a storm as his bare head,*" she murmurs, rocking back on her heels.

"*In hell black night endures,*" Gloucester takes up liturgically, spacing each word out rigidly, each with equal emphasis. He needs no prompting now, he knows the lines. He has always known them. They have been there from the time of his birth.

" ... *would have buoyed up*
And quenched stelled fires;
Yet, poor old heart, he help the heaven to rain.
If wolves, if wolves ..."

"*At the gate*," Regan murmurs coaxingly.

" ... *howled that dern time*," Gloucester says, working grimly through the fatal syllables, seeing ahead, like a milestone in the distance, the final two lines of the speech.

"*Thou shouldst have said, 'Good porter turn the key,'*" Gloucester says slowly, turning ponderously at the end of the line for the next, the first of his final two lines.

"*All cruels else subscribed: but I shall see*," Gloucester looks ahead.

It is an impossibly long way to the end of the line.

Lear is hissing from behind the curtain, but it is a steep slope ahead for Gloucester, full of snarling faces with animal snouts.

Easier to let go and fall. With gravity. He's heard that gravity is simply the curvature of space around a massive object. Very well, let him fall; let him slide the gravitational curve.

"... *and we shall see*," he enunciates clearly, "*Winged vengeance overtake such children.*"

He spits in Regan's face.

"Tread on his eyes," Cornwall shouts in a travesty of his real lines. His eyes are bulging out from his head and his lower lip is quivering.

Gloucester turns away and tried to drag his chair out of Regan's reach. Extra, Fleance and I grab the chair and try to drag it around to face the audience.

"*He that will think to live to be old,*
Give me some help!"

Regan's fingers hover a few inches from his eyes; the long, sybaritic curve of her nails occupies his entire visual field.

They flash in the light.

"*O cruel. O ye gods.*" A scream from Gloucester.

Cornwall dances up and down. "*Out vile jelly*," he screams, hopelessly out of place. "*Where is thy lustre now?*"

Another scream from Gloucester. Extra, Fleance and I struggle to hold down the chair. Regan is panting as if she has run a long way. She gazes around the stage exultantly.

Paint splashes onto the stage.

"*One side will mock the other*," Regan announces.

I draw my sword ready to attack Cornwall. Regan's hands flash again.

Abruptly the stage goes quiet. Gloucester stands up slowly, the ropes falling from him. His hands are over his face and there is red dripping from between his fingers.

"*All dark*," he intones vibrantly. "*All dark and comfortless.*" He is facing the audience.

I have never heard him deliver the lines so well.

Lear is running onto the stage, Cordelia following. Still Curan and Extra don't understand what has happened. Extra grabs hold of Curan's arm.

"Stab Cornwall!" she shouts.

The Fool is running beside Lear.

"*Mark it, nuncle, mark it!*" he screeches.

Oswald passes Curan, heading for a spot in the audience. "Flee, Curan," he says quietly.

"*Let him smell his way to Dover*," Regan snarls.

Lear grips Gloucester. His face has withered to the blank stupidity of a baby. All his magnificent stage presence has gone; his whole body has shrunk. Is this Lear? Am I Curan?

Gloucester shakes him off and scrabbles around the floor of the stage, one hand covering his face, the other feeling in the rough grass.

"Not here, not there. Look in the pockets of your doublets. Lost and Found. I can't find them," voice rising in hysteria. "When I open them they aren't there. Where are you, Mainchance?" He peers forward, a lookout in a crow's nest. "Once I was a sailor, a river life for me." He peers to the right and the left. A tide of dark lit with bolts of colour. That would be ruptured nerve endings. "We knew it would happen, didn't we Mainchance? A sail! A sail!"

Something after all. An audience. A shape, a flicker. A flicker in the shape. A curling line. A figure. A figure with a hood and human face, hidden, standing right next to him.

"Look out, Mainchance!" his voice rises and falls as he pulls each word out of shape, bending the vowels beyond recognition. "There's one beside you now. And it's hungry." He giggles.

"It's very hungry."

Curan runs. Leaping out towards the audience, past the boy and girl and the cluster at the front, through the frozen, waxen figures that sit in ranks behind them. More blobs of flesh and colour whose bodies are stiff scarecrows. Up to the back lip of the amphitheatre and into the forest, a shadow among shadows, not pausing once (step on a crack you marry a rat) until the shadows have enclosed her. Crouching down to make herself as invisible as possible.

Don't breathe.

Among the ferns and shadows I will never be seen. I turn back to the stage. And look.

Lear's sword is out.

"Gloucester!" he roars, as if Gloucester were many miles away.

Gloucester turns his back to him.

"Mainchance!" he shouts in the other direction.

Lear wants to swear vengeance. That the mocking world would right itself at the tip of his blade. He opens his mouth to swear but no words come out. He cannot get past the first letter of Gloucester's name.

"G-g-g-g-g-g-g-g."

With enormous effort he gets to the l:

"L-l-l-l-l-l-l-l,"

It is going to take him many years to swear eternal vengeance.

He begs; let it come down. Nothing left but bones, fossils and specimens.

Clawing and screaming, Cordelia throws herself at Regan. Regan's fingers leap gratefully towards Cordelia's face; the bones crack as they connect with Cordelia's knuckles.

Sword drawn, Lear approaches the two women, parrying as if with an invisible enemy, circling them and searching for a clever thrust.

Edmund, who vanished off stage in the commotion, appears leading Albany. Albany's knees are rubbery and Edmund is holding him by the scruff of his neck. When he sees Lear and the fighting women he drops Albany and skips lightly to the front of the stage. He bows deeply at the audience, smiling to left and right, before making a comical show of creeping up behind Lear. With exaggerated stealth he stalks his prey, sometimes tripping up over his own feet.

Lear turns and takes a swing at him. Edmund easily evades, letting the sword pass a few safe inches from his arm, gaping at the audience with mock alarm. The Fool jumps up to Lear.

"*Here's grace and a cod-piece; that's a wise man and a fool.*"

Edmund slips behind Lear and seizes his arms, twisting one up his back and the other, with the sword, high in the air. Edmund's face twists with mock strain.

The sword falls to the ground.

"Over here, nuncle," Edmund says jovially, dragging Lear over to the lantern at stage left. "Every dog has its day, nuncle. Is that in the play? We'll have a roast for your highness any moment now." He bows to Lear, still holding him with one hand. "We'll have the slaves bring it in. Only be a moment. It's a small matter of taming the sauce." To Cornwall he says, "Be nimble, lad, bring the rope that's sleeping by the chair; we'll truss the hams."

Cornwall shambles over with the rope. He stares at it before giving it to Edmund. His fingers are bloody.

"Now Edmund, the blood's freezing in my veins. It's all icy on my hands." He rubs his hands on the grass.

"Any moment now," Edmund says heartily. "We'll sup with the nobles of Babylon. And their ladies. Isn't that what you wanted, nuncle? Can you hear the applause? The crowd is on its feet." He rubs Lear's ears energetically. "Can you hear it? There is still time to take a bow, make a turn or two about the stage, catch the eye of a pretty girl in the front row," he catches the eye of the tawny-haired girl and grins his big Edmund grin. "There's one at every show; isn't that right, nuncle?"

He bends over Lear who is doubled over from the pain in his arms.

"That's right, bow low, nuncle." As he speaks he secures Lear's wrists behind his back and pulls the rope tight. He fastens it to the lantern pole, whistling the theme to 'My Sweet Lesbia' by Thomas Campion.

The Fool leans over Lear.

"*Thou wouldst make a good fool,*" he shouts, skirting away from Edmund's warning fist.

Lear closes his eyes and screws them shut. Nothing. *Nothing will come of nothing*. Lear said that.

"Gloucester!" he roars, finally breaking open his teeth for the syllables. The sound is carried away in the dark tide. Fallen, fallen. Alas Babylon!

Edmund saunters over to where Regan and Cordelia are fighting, leaving Lear to struggle against his bonds. Cordelia has a hold of Regan's rich, dark hair and is pulling her backwards by the neck. Regan screeches like a parrot and claws at Cordelia's face. Edmund grins gloatingly at them, turning to the audience with a shrug.

Seeing him, Cordelia tries to pull away and Regan's fingers find the fabric of her white Ophelia gown which rips down the front. Edmund chuckles and circles behind her with the same exaggerated movements with which he stalked Lear.

Grimly, Cordelia swings away from him, Regan still hanging on. In a few seconds the three of them are whirling, Cordelia swinging around the axis of Regan, trying to pull free, while Edmund, whooping and yipping, tries to catch Cordelia.

In Curan's eyes the three blur, blending into a single rotating entity. A creature of whirlwinds.

Edmund stops and turns in the reverse direction, flinging his arms out histrionically for Cordelia, who is flung into them. He pins her arms up behind her as he did with Lear, whistling between his teeth. With a flourish he takes a piece of rope and ties the knot, breaking into song. His is a light, pleasant baritone:

" 'Now what is love, I pray thee, tell?

It is that fountain and that well

Where pleasure and repentance dwell.'"

Is that a lute Curan can hear, behind the curtain?

Cordelia kicks hard, trying to connect with his shins, but he avoids her deftly, doing a comical dance and grinning over his shoulder at the audience who have gone on watching events as if it were still the play.

" 'It is perhaps that sauncing bell

That tolls all into heaven or to hell.'"

Regan is panting hard. There's a welt of blood on her cheek where her face has been scratched.

"Let me have her, Edmund" she says shortly. Edmund bows to her and sings lustily:

" 'Now what is love, I pray thee sayen

It is the sunshine mixed with rain

It is a gentle pleasing pain.'"

"*Here's a night pities neither wise man nor fool,*" The Fool remarks, examining Lear's bonds.

"Untie me," Lear says reasonably. The Fool shies away.

"*They'll have me whipped. Mark it, nuncle. I'd rather be any kind o' thing than a Fool.*" He draws an imaginary blade across his throat. "*So out went the candle and we were left darkling.*"

At Edmund's bidding Cornwall brings the stocks. Edmund measures the hole with thumb and forefinger, then makes a show of measuring Cordelia's wrists. He shouts across to Lear, "Which is the rounder or most fulsome, nuncle, the legs of a skinny dwarf, or the arms of a woman?"

Holding Cordelia almost delicately by one hand he forces her to the ground, her arms above her head, wrists locked in the stocks which are in turn tied to the lantern pole at stage right.

" 'Now what is love I pray thee show?
A thing that creeps, it cannot go
A prize that passeth to and fro
A thing for one, a thing for moe
And he that prove shall find it so.'"

Kent stalks Gloucester in the night. How far can a blind man have wandered? Not far; blundering off to one side of the stage in fact, feeling his way along the wall of the church, wailing, "*Away, let me die, let me die,*" pausing occasionally to declaim, "*Where's my son, Edmund? Edmund, enkindle all the sparks of nature to quit his horrid act.*"

What a huge stage! Spread in all directions and lost in an infinity of indigo and steel. The sky. The sky? What whirling things are these? Are stars a myth? We look backwards in time, don't we, Mainchance, when we look at the stars? When did you last see the stars? We ride, bareback, the photon wave; it's for gamblers, the law of probability. Blind chance. Ha ha ha ha ha ha. And the applause! It comes from all sides like the rushing of water, the beating of angel's wings. Can you hear it, Mainchance? Throw them some couplets. A rhyme or thrice. A bouquet of lines. Or lilies. Lilies or lines. That puts a reverse into the difference. Something to echo around the universe. How far can a lily shout?

Now let's see.

He sings:

"*As flies to wanton boys, are we to the gods;*
They kill us for their sport."

It doesn't rhyme? That's opposite. It's opposite that it's opposite. This is blank verse. I strongly advise you to read Bradley and Wilson Knight, Mainchance. Balance! Redress! That is the gambler's hope. No die can stand on its end. The ball falls to its rightful socket.

There's someone approaching. What ho, friend or foe? I am blind for want of eyes. Ha ha. The applause comes only once. The tread again, light on the turf.

"*Away, get thee away; good friend, be gone;*
All thy comforts can do me no good at all."

Kent stops a few yards from him. "*You cannot see your way,*" he says softly, adopting the tones of Edgar.

Gloucester turns in the direction of his voice.

"*I have no way and therefore want no eyes.*
Who's there? Tis poor mad Tom."

No, wait. Those lines belong to Extra or Curan, whoever plays the Old Man. What if he were to forget his lines now? Is Curan behind the curtain? Or Mainchance? Ah, he begins to recite:

"*There's a cliff, whose high and bending head*
Looks fearfully in the confined deep;
Bring me but to the brim of it
And I'll, I'll . . ."

He pauses to listen to Curan's whispered voice. The sequence is clear in his mind now, even if the words have become a little jumbled. Edgar will lead him, not to the high cliffs of Dover, but to a mere rill in the ground. Believing he is throwing himself off a high cliff, Gloucester will fall. Edgar, in another disguise, will pretend to rescue him from the bottom of the cliff, describing the fiend who led him there. That's all in the script. But Gloucester is tired. Very tired. Perhaps a short rest before that exhausting scene.

"Good Edgar, return me to the barge. I'm fatally weary. The circle is broken and the dark rushes in to fill up all available space. Nature abhors a vacuum. A seething mass of virtual particles, Edgar, for what the eye would construe. It replaces the marrow in the bones. I never was an actor, but I believe Gloucester has all the apposite lines. *One side will mock the other*, she said. O dreadful symmetry! Horrible balance! Even half the world is better than none when both go wanting. Better *I were distract*. My eyes bound with flax and the whites of eggs.

"*So should my thoughts be severed from my griefs*
And woes by wrong imaginations lose
The knowledge of themselves …"

Kent (still in the voice of Edgar): "*Give me your hand.*"

"Come hither, Dukes," Edmund shouts, "You know your parts. Or you should. You've been handling them long enough." He giggles. Regan taps her foot.

"Don't piss around, Edmund," she snaps. Edmund gestures to Cornwall and Albany.

"Her legs, you pigswill. Hold them down." He takes out his tin and rattles it, rolling his eyes until only the whites show.

Albany has raised himself onto one elbow and is staring stupidly at the tin box. Cornwall falls clumsily onto Cordelia's legs. Albany gets up and crosses the stage. He looks down at the bound and struggling Cordelia.

"No," he says slowly. Suddenly he makes a wild grab for the tin which

Edmund snatches away.

"Get to it, Albany," says Regan, "our patience is wearing thin."

"Pace, Albany, pace," Edmund declaims, waving an imaginary stick, glancing across at Lear.

Albany backs away.

"I don't want any part of it." At a certain distance he stops and looks brokenly at Edmund. He lacks the courage to go forward or back.

"Come on baby, pretty baby," Cornwall sings in a high, childlike voice. He is sitting on one of Cordelia's knees, staring up anxiously at Albany. "Don't be a naughty boy now or we'll both be in the poo. You don't want to land in the poo."

Albany shuffles a few steps forward.

"It will be alright, won't it?" he asks Cornwall timidly. "I'm frightened. A very frightened boy. I've been frightened for a long time."

"Of course it's alright, baby," Cornwall croons, glancing at Edmund who nods encouragingly. "You'll feel much better in a minute."

Edmund takes Albany's hand and leads him formally around Cordelia's feet. He points to her leg.

"All you have to do is sit here," he says in a kindly voice.

He holds down Cordelia's foot while Albany climbs gingerly on. Cordelia heaves against the weight of the two men, but eventually falls limp. Edmund gives Albany a tablet. Albany stares at the tiny pill, then swallows it. Edmund gets up and makes a gesture of dusting himself off, blowing on his fingertips. He gives a tablet to Cornwall. Where's poor Tom?

"The Death is on you, Edmund," Cordelia says distinctly.

"We'll hear your voice in good time," Edmund says.

To Lear, the Fool says,

"*Let the great gods*
That keep this dreadful pother o'er our heads
Find out their enemies now."

Lear screws his eyes shut until the pressure on his eyeballs makes him dizzy. Lightning on the dark. Surely no bonds can hold me nor chains lock the flesh.

"Untie my bonds," he says to the Fool in the same reasonable voice. A reasonable request to make of any soul.

Edmund bends down and picks up Lear's sword, waving it aloft with a flourish. He bows to Lear, the audience, and finally Regan, who watches him unblinkingly. He eases the Dukes apart with his foot and delicately cuts Cordelia's Ophelia gown from neck to leg. He stands back to consider the effect, nodding to himself.

Cordelia begins to scream. It is an eerie pervasive sound that seems to rise not just from her throat but from the whole stage, saturating the air, floating by Curan as if it were coming from the trees. It is a high coasting note, full of detached horror. When it ceases Edmund turns to Regan.

"She's yours," he says negligently.

Edgar peers at the scene from behind the back curtain. It is clear to him that the para-beings have taken over the stage. The reality of it comes as a shock to him; while he's toyed with the idea, teased it out for what it was worth, underneath he's thought of it as just a folk legend - a way to scare children at night. It is one thing to dream about them in the forest, quite another to meet them on the human stage in the guise of people he knows well.

The para-beings are real and walk the earth.

Either that or he is still sitting in the church, candle glowing between his knuckles, and the jewelled bird has not returned him to his true time. There is an annoying dark spot in his vision he cannot account for. It was never there before. A tiny black speck that settles into whatever he focuses upon.

No. He can discard that sliver of fear. He has known the agony of re-entering the flesh; knowing once again his intolerable love. He peers out beyond the stage to the night, beyond the audience still gaping at the stage, his eyes, searching out the gloom for the glint of the river. This is the world of humankind, yet man has had his dominion. The forest pushes the thin huddle of huts towards the river; the cogs of a new reality close in on each other, and humankind is squeezed between them like a pip. He watches the par-Regan kneel worshipfully between Cordelia's legs. The movement is careful, gentle, like a considerate lover. And the pip goes spinning through space far from its accustomed home. Wheeee! *Star blasting and taking.*

The para-being lifts her head from between Cordelia's thighs and grins at Edmund, her lips blurring together. What did the bird say? Allow her embrace and your blood will turn to dust. Looking at Regan with cool, scientific detachment, Edgar understands the nature of the para-beings more thoroughly than his earlier speculations had allowed. They are no imitations, but rather one with the flesh of their victims. Regan is still Regan. He should remember that fact.

Again, like a lioness at her prey, Regan's head lowers, apparently with infinite slowness, back between Cordelia's thighs. Regan, halfling; a dream formed between the passions of the mind and the will of the earth.

How he could make up speeches now, if he had the stage! He could best the pen of the Bard and out-word the world. It could take the form of a hymn to Curan. Curan the Beautiful, Curan the Flighty, Curan the Cruel. The Deadly.

Look! The dew forms threads on her skin. *Tom's a cold.*

Lear turns to the Fool. "*Nature's above art in that respect.*" He strains his head towards Regan. "*Look a mouse. Peace. Peace. A piece of toasted cheese will do it.*"

The Fool nods his clown's head. "*She will taste like this as a crab does to a crab.*"

Lear nods in unison.

"It will come," he says with solemnity.

"*Humanity must perforce prey on itself*

Like monsters of the deep."

Something peculiar begins to happen to Curan's vision. She is seeing these events through a screen. Some sort of filter. Globes of light float back and forth across the field, bouncing clumsily off the ground, turning the scene first one colour, then another. It is as if they are under a giant crystal flower moving to a lazy wind.

Goneril wanders onto the stage, lute in hand, arms rotating in slow motion as if she is swimming. As she passes in front of the lantern where Lear is tied she goes transparent; Curan is able to see through her flesh, through her muscles and blood vessels. Her body is glowing red, a swaying balloon filled with blood. Curan can see into her womb and the shape of her foetus. She is near term and it is almost fully developed. She sees the sleek head of a rat and the body of a fish. The rat looks at her and bares its teeth; its tail jerks spasmodically in the confined space. Its face is narrow and hairy, the body appears almost recessive. There are sharp scales running down its backbone.

Goneril crosses the stage and squats down on the stocks, near Cordelia's head and strums a chord on her lute.

"I'm undecided," she announces to the audience, "whether to sing 'Sleep, Wayward Thoughts' by John Dowland, or 'Down, Down, Proud Mind' By William Corkine".

Regan looks up, pokes out her tongue and wriggles it at Goneril.

"How about the Corkine song," she says from the back of her throat. "It's one of my favourites."

Goneril sings:

" 'Down, down proud mind
Thou soarest far above thy might
Aspiring heart wilt thou not cease to breed my woe?
Thoughts meet with disdain
Peace and love fight
Peace thou hast won the field

And love shall hence in bondage go.'"

"Don't listen to her, Fool," Lear babbles. "She has the voice of a magpie. When she walks she dances like a duck. She's a vulture. Her words are sweet but tucked hard against the skull. We'll cut our lips to pieces on such songs. When she eats, the flesh comes off in ribbons. *Nature's above art in that respect.* You'll recall. *Ay, every inch a king.* You'll swallow that. Where's Kent? He has his inches. Ha ha. You'll swallow that one. I'll not cry but shrink first. Vanish 'til I am no bigger than a fart's fingernail. Ha ha! I'll not cry but transmute my tears into malady. Ratsbane and vulpicide. You'll swallow that. Fool enough for you, Fool? Let's find Edgar or a good apothecary. Either will do. Untie me now Fool that I might seek them out."

The Fool steps a pace backward, hangs his foolish head.

"For the love of God untie me, and I'll dispatch these demons back to hell."

The Fool takes a further step back, stops and scratches his head.

"*The trick of the voice I do well remember,*" he says in Gloucester's voice. "*I'st not the king?*"

Edmund stands at the front of the stage, peering out towards the audience. The boy and the girl are still there, having moved back a little, eyes avid for the stage. There is a restless movement among the rest of the audience; a whisper, like wind passing over wheat. An uneasy shifting.

Edmund will soon settle them in.

He takes off his shirt and the bird comes alive, looking out over the field with a sharp, predatory interest. (Curan ducks). Absently he strokes its wings, whispering softly. Grandly, as if doing a conjurer's trick, he removes his trousers.

Once naked, he parades across the stage, thrusting out his crotch and making sharp, yipping noises. He begins to rotate his shoulders, putting the bird into cumbersome flight. He moves quietly at first but then with increasing tempo. His cock has grown so large it appears to be pushing up against the bird's tail, seeking entry.

There is a hail of applause in his ears. He turns gleefully to Lear. "Can you hear it, nuncle?" Show them, show them! He rotates his crotch, moving it rhythmically against his chest, his cock sliding in and out of the bird's tail feathers. He sustains this circular movement through Goneril's next verse.

" 'This fall from pride
My rising is from grief's great deep
That bottom wants up to the top of happy bliss
In peace and rest I shall securely sleep
Where neither scorn, disdain, loves torment,
Grief or anguish is.' "

Clapping his hands above his head in a victory salute, Edmund walks back to where Cordelia is lying.

"*O well flown bird!*" sings Lear, trying to dance in his bonds. "*Let copulation thrive. The fitchew nor the soiled horse go to it with more riotous appetite.*"

Edmund nods gravely in Lear's direction and stoops over to lift Regan from between Cordelia's legs. Regan's head lolls to one side, her body limp. Lifting her legs to avoid Albany, he rolls her over near Cordelia. Cornwall and Albany are giggling, holding hands.

At last she lies before him, spread out like a rabbit stew, just as he has prophesied; Regan, like a true wife, having warmed her up a little.

Everything is complete. I have to follow this through now, Edmund thinks lucidly. I have no choice.

He stretches across her body, supporting himself with his arms. He is poised above her; at no point does his body touch hers. The bird flexes its wings, the talons shiver.

Slowly he brings his crotch to meet hers.

Kent says, "I'll take you to the barge, uncle. You can sleep or dream all you wish. The time has come for that. The leopard and the panther join our company." Bending down, Kent scoops up a stick and holds it out to Gloucester. If Gloucester takes his hand he will certainly recognize the dwarf.

"I'm sorry, uncle, I have the Sickness hard upon me and may not take your arm. Follow my voice and hold on to the stick."

Gloucester grasps the stick.

"Describe it to me, Edgar, as we move along." What was that about riding the photon wave? Instead he's shuffling along like an old blind man with only his loyal son to guide him. This way it will take him many lifetimes to reach paradise. A comfortless road. The gestures of dark.

"It is a golden city. A city full of gleaming spires and endless markets; avenues of cypresses and lilies. There are graceful colonnades where stroll kings and princes. Now of course the city is sleeping, its streets slick with moonlight, but for the theatre-goers who will see the dawn. The sky is as sharp as glass with stars you can hold in your eye. The gardens are silent; the roses are purple under the moon.

"We are passing through a deserted square at the centre of which is a fountain. No water runs, but there is water as in a still pond. There are rubies and diamonds glinting at the bottom of the fountain, but no-one has attempted to claim them due to the legend that the waters of the fountain will peel the flesh from the bone."

"I'm thirsty," says Gloucester, "for real water. And I must wash my poor old eyes. My face aches. My body is a knot of pain."

"Soon, soon," Kent says hastily. "On the barge rosewater and balm are being prepared. Soft oils and gauzes for your wounds. Listen to my description and follow as fast as you are able.

"Naked youths ride the backs of animals, rich-scented wine flows the streets and a great feast is in preparation to celebrate the play. None of this the audience sees, Gloucester, for their eyes are fixed on that thin page of light where we Players move and give our lines. They are trapped in our bewitchment. Meanwhile the city unfolds in the moonlight like loaves of fresh white bread." Kent swallows noisily.

"Ah! The barge. Our dear old *Earl of Southampton*, bedecked with flowers which are heaped so high they tumble off into the water and are carried away by the dark stream." He snatches up some weeds growing by the side of the path and holds them near Gloucester's nose. "But still they go on heaping them up. Can't you smell them, uncle?"

"I believe I can, Edgar," Gloucester stops. "Strange, I have no pain. My face feels washed clean. What kind of miracle is this?"

Kent tugs at the stick. "It's the cleansing effect of the flowers, Gloucester. Their very scent has a healing effect." He waves the weeds under Gloucester's nose again. "We are passing gardens laid out in exquisite designs, each part reflecting the whole; a cunning tribute to the landscaper's art. Fields of roses so densely packed they appear as lakes. Asphodels wave near grottos; there are violets, poppies and narcissus in a collage of colour. Tame leopards and panthers with velvet hides pad softly among the garden plots, their eyes gleaming." Kent closes his eyes to shut out the hovels and shacks they are passing.

A thin wail goes up from the stage, and dies away. Gloucester stops.

"It's only the cry of lovers," Kent says quickly, "That here and there embrace in the gardens, under the honeysuckle and the rose, letting go their pleasure. There are protected arbours and tiny summer houses ideal for the purpose." He tugs on the stick.

Gloucester sighs and shuffles forward.

"Strange, Edgar, it sounded like a woman drowning far away. One of your flowers, perhaps, ha ha; a nice conceit. The cycle is almost complete. I've grown gills for lungs. I've played my part, faithfully. I've delivered my lines. Carried out my commission. Mainchance will have to carry it from now on. Let him find my eyes, if he can. Food for rats! A rare delicacy, Edgar, for a rodent palate."

"Soon you will be lying down amongst petals and nosegays. You will want for nothing. Your every whim pampered. The play is almost done."

Gloucester sighs more deeply than before.

"This is a very happy day for me, Edgar," he says solemnly. He stops. "No-one can take that away from me."

"That's right," Kent says, pulling on the stick. "That's a very courageous way of looking at it, Gloucester. We're nearly there. Take care with the planking of the wharf."

"I've been a fool for too long," Gloucester says wonderingly.

Curan burrows deeper into the floor of the forest. I am a burrowing creature, a being of fern and moss, a creature of twigs and leaves. Look at me and I vanish before your eyes. I am one with the dirt, and my home is here among the blind burrowing creatures. I can breathe with the trees, send my roots down deep into the warm places of the earth, exhale the mineral breath of rock.

At the same time I am planning, quite cold-bloodedly, how to kill Edmund. With Edmund dead we will have a happy Company and Regan will grow into her goodness. I could even love her then, even now, after all this. It will not be difficult to kill Edmund; it is simply a matter of waiting my time. My hands are murderer's hands.

Calmly I look back at the stage.

I have to follow it now, see it to the very end, sure in the knowledge that I can kill Edmund. That Death will serve me. That I will kill Regan also, if I have to. How easy those deaths seem to me. How glibly I can visualize them. And how deep I burrow into my black lover, the earth, whose warm roots entwine me.

As Edmund rotates his hips the bird appears to grow. Its wings, which once extended only across his chest, have spread over his shoulders and down his arms. His whole body ripples as if taking flight as the globes of light swing across him. Again and again the bird dips its beak into Cordelia's breast. A trickle of blood flows down Edmund's navel. He arches his back, his head lifting upwards, the cords of his neck standing out.

He's dying, Curan thinks.

The bird leers over the forest.

"Cut me loose, fool of a Fool," Lear whispers brokenly, "But once cut me loose and I'll drag it back to hell myself for my own soul's perdition."

The Fool dances, juggling invisible balls.

"*There's hell and darkness, there's the sulphurous pit. Burning, scalding,*" he clutches his crotch, "*Stench consumption; fie fie fie! Pah pah! Give me an ounce of civet, good apothecary, to sweeten my imagination.*"

"I know those lines," Lear says slowly. "They're mine."

Each time the bird lifts from Cordelia's breast its piercing eye seeks out Curan in her hiding place among the roots and leaves. It looks straight at her. It wants to land on her and lift her up into the sky. Regan is lying by Cordelia, her head only a few inches from the reach of the other woman. She is apparently inert, head rolled to one side, but I notice that her eyes are open, bright and glassy like the eyes of the corpse.

As soon as I see them her fingers curl and I double up in agony. I grip onto the roots of the tree. I call on its strength to flow into me. My fingers scrabble in the leaves.

With patient cunning Edgar devises his strategy. He will join the para-beings and pass among them as one of them. If they see through his disguise and devour him his deception will have been well worth its folly. If not, he may find Curan and in finding, embrace; and in embracing, penetrate; and in that violation flower his death.

He hunches over and throws his neck out the way a bird does. He moves his head quickly this way and that. Picking up his feet like a stick-legged water bird, he makes his way across to the winged creature that crouches over Cordelia.

"*Tom's a cold,*" he croaks, "*Tom's a cold,*" How like a bird cry it sounds, he thinks, bending over to examine the Dukes who are still straddled across Cordelia's legs, twined in a rapturous kiss.

"*Tom's a cold,*" he repeats, moving closer to the bird. He can hear the rattle of a familiar tin in amongst its plumage. The bird looks his way and says something unintelligible, probably in its own language, Edgar decides. It then turns its head back and forth rapidly, each eye leaping in turn out towards the forest.

Next he tries Goneril, who's moved to the very side of the stage and is sitting under the lantern at stage right, softly strumming her lute.

"*Tom's a cold. Tom's a cold,*" he chants. He falls onto his knees and tries to crawl under her dress. Ample room here for a Curan to make herself small and hide. But there is no room. The way is blocked by a huge egg. Softly she sings an Elizabethan lyric and Edgar listens to the words, knowing she is singing them just for him. He recognizes the tune, 'In Sherwood Forest Lived Stout Robin Hood.'

" ' … leave we the woods behind us.

Love's passions must not be withstood,

Love everywhere will find us.

I lived in a field and town, and so did he;

I got me to the woods; love followed me.'"

In the forest. Curan? 'Love followed me'. How could he find her out there?

He turns to Regan who is lying nearby and bends, birdlike, over her. Her eyes are open and her pupils have dilated so completely they've swallowed the irises. She makes clawing motions with her fingers, her mouth opening and closing. As it opens he notices swarms of black flies emerging. Examining closer he sees her tongue caked in blood.

It's that jewelled bird, back in the church; it sent me to this dreadful place, he thinks. It lied to me, that bird. It really did kill me. Then it sent me here. If I go down to the river and throw myself under its oily skin I'll simply be washed back up here, in this place - what did the bird call it? A hole. It was mocking me. If I am dead, then let it be unhinged.

Still in his bird disguise he hops over to Lear and the Fool. It is important to keep his rational processes working.

"*Here's a spirit*," the Fool says to Lear as he approaches.

Edgar nods an acknowledgement to the Fool.

"My Lord, by your leave," he says to Lear, "I seek Curan the Courtier. Not Curan of the warm flesh, you understand, but she whose flesh is leaves and grass and that which burrows and rots. The flesh that stinks of graves; this flesh, grave flesh, flesh of earth and cold winds, thorn and twisted fruit. Flesh of water and every scuttling hunger. Makeshift Curan from the dreams of sucking. *Bless thy five wits*. Curan who casts no shadow; the one who walks behind her."

"*Behold yon simpering dame,*" Lear shouts,
Whose face between her forks presageth snow;
That minces virtue, and does shake her head
To hear of pleasure's name…

"Come, good Edgar, unfumble these bonds, a mere twist of fingers will do the job and Lear is restored. We'll have graves enough for your liking soon."

"*Tom's a cold*," says Edgar, hoping to learn more.

"Stay clear!" Lear shouts. "Here a whirlwind lies shag with the earth. The leaf turns on infinity. I should have run him through this morning. When the sharp steel pricked the fiend's eye. Aye! She stopped me. She put her lips against my opal brooch. Is that fool enough for you, Fool? *Strip thine own back*. Scrape the flesh out. Untie me while there's still a world for knots."

Edgar hops away, "*Tom's a cold, Tom's a cold.*" There is no sense to be had out of Lear. His wits have gone foolish and the Fool keeps him company. Not for Edgar.

183

The Fool skips after him.

"*Let not the creaking of shoes nor the rustling of silks betray thy poor heart to women; keep thy foot out of Brothels, thy hand out of plackets, and defy the foul fiend.*"

They are Edgar's lines.

The bird has begun to flap its wings, as if to rise and take clumsy flight. Then, like a rope parting, the bird is gone and Edmund sprawls heavily across Cordelia his lips stretched back across his teeth, screaming, as Cordelia rips a chunk of flesh from his shoulder. She coughs it out to get another.

Edmund leaps back, his face twisted in fury, blood rushing from the wound. He turns, snarling, to Lear.

"We'll have to take the heat out of the guts."

"*You do wrong to take me out of the grave*," Lear shouts to him. "*I will not swear these are my hands.*" He turns to the retreating Edgar. "Untie me, Edgar, and you will be a saint for life. My Fool has been turned into a chicken who squawks for lack of a head. I know your fingers will not want for wit, good Edgar; you have played your part with valour and discretion. Untie me and I'll prick these maggots to bursting."

"*Tom will throw his head at them*," Edgar shouts back as he follows Edmund who has run off the stage. "*Avaunt you curs!*" he hops like a bird, as if chasing after Edmund, but Edmund is already returning to the stage, leading Caliban.

Edgar stops at the sight of the ape. The beast's eyes pass across him indifferently. At that moment he sees Curan, lying on the ground, her face covered in dirt, her fingers gripping the earth like pale roots. It is the same picture he saw during his time of darkness and walking. He realizes that what he is seeing is an elaborate construct, a para-world, a precise holographic imitation. Yet he is sure Curan is there, just as he sees her. To this extent the para-world reflects the nature of the world he lives and moves in; something strung together with words and symbols;

something to be acted out, nightly, in a hundred places like Babylon. The key is there, imbedded runically in the act. Hold on to the right and true path. It is a long thread and leads directly to Curan. His love; the anguish of his secret.

Edmund leads Caliban onto the stage and once around for applause. He produces a large, heavy ball - presto! - and Caliban is induced to walk on top of it, dancing first on one foot then the other, beating on his chest with his fists. Edmund walks beside him, ready to lend a hand. He has thrown a cloak over the wound on his shoulder.

Goneril strums her lute.

Caliban is escorted by Edmund to where Cordelia is lying, the Dukes still straddling her, wrapped in each other's arms. Holding on to Caliban's lead, he bends over and says something to the Dukes, taking out his tin and rattling it.

"It's a big breakthrough for us, Edmund," Albany says. "We've always done it to each other but we could never kiss. No kissing, that was the rule. We were afraid of the Sickness, afraid of everything. We fed off our fears. We've overcome that."

"I'm very happy for you," Edmund says pleasantly, "Now shift your carcasses and let the monkey smell the bait."

Albany continues, "It's a big thing to get over. To kiss each other. To exchange tenderness." His tongue lolls heavily in his mouth, obstructing his words.

Edmund nods sympathetically.

"Now help me roll her over lads, Caliban doesn't like the missionary position. It never caught on. He prefers 'em sunny side up."

"We've got a lot to thank you for, Edmund," Albany says sincerely, "We really have."

Cordelia's voice is heard faintly.

"*How does my Lord, how fares your majesty?*
... O look upon me, sir,

And hold your benediction o'er me.
No sir, you must not kneel.

"They are motes in the air, without substance, without fire; they throw no ghost on the glass when they breathe. In all the world there are but deserts and mountains for men to walk upon. Do you know that time? Set your crown straight. *Every inch a king*, upright by the habit of command. Set your crown straight. Your brooch remembers the sunlight, Lord; its light is our slow glass. Save me! Hold me! Time shuts its knife on us. Hold me!"

Edmund: "Be patient, sweety. Succour is on its way." He forces the beast down. Caliban moves his head from side to side uncertainly.

"A lot of men have that hang up," Albany says. "It's not so much a question of sex but of tenderness and love. There is a French word for it, *tendresse*."

"I'll believe you," Edmund says, concentrating. He reaches down under Cordelia then holds his fingers up to the animal's nose, at the same time taking a firm hold of its member, stroking it and talking softly.

"There, my beauty, even a dog may have the scraps that fall from the table. A bone to lick clean. Isn't that right, nuncle?" He urges the animal, "Forward, forward!"

Caliban's hips begin to pump jerkily.

Lear is babbling to an invisible spirit on his left. At the same time his eyes roll regularly around towards the Fool.

"*A man may see how this world goes without eyes*. Gloucester says that, the Fool confirms it. The ayes have it. They always have. It's the habit of command, ha ha. We are shaped by a caprice. I am bound to answer, Fool, but being bound can give no answer. This is a riddle, Fool, only you can loosen. It's on the nose. An honest troupe of players, sir. An honest play. And we, sir, have neither the reason to lose wits nor the wits to lose reason. There's logic for you, Fool. As long as we hold on to our fingers. It's a wise Fool who knows the difference between a knot and a bow -

untie me, Fool - between rope and gossamer and daisy chain. These are but garlands about my wrists." The Fool edges closer, glancing fearfully towards Edmund.

"She loves me, she loves me not," Lear sings, his eyes on the Fool. "Poor flower to lose its petals so. She loves me and the world's redeemed, Fool. Such bonds show not in the wrist. Can't the wisdom of a Fool unbind them? Hurry, sirrah!"

With a swift movement the Fool releases Lear who staggers across the stage towards Edmund.

"*Kill kill kill kill kill kill!*"

Edmund dances lithely back, deftly tripping Lear who sprawls across Cordelia's ankles.

"Wait your turn, nuncle," says Edmund gaily. "The Dukes will entertain you for the while. I'll hold this calf down myself."

He scoops up Lear's sword and hands it to Cornwall before turning back to Caliban.

"Have you forgotten," the Fool shouts after Lear, "*Let copulation thrive... Down from the waist they are Centaurs, though all woman above.*"

Cornwall levels the sword at Lear's breast. It trembles and goes steady. A hard, murderous look comes across Cornwall's face.

"You've always despised us, haven't you, *king*? You have admitted that much, right?"

Lear begins to dance. An awkward, clumsy, bear-like dance: and sings in a cracked, hoarse voice,

"Trust a wolf to deliver a pig,

We'll add some garlic and some fig.

"Goneril, your lute! Music! Let's play, 'Come Again Sweet Love Doth Now Invite.' How does it go? 'By sighs and tears more hot than thy shafts,' a gentle piece." He hops from one side to the other. "I'll not cry again 'til we're sheeted in blood, murdered blood. We'll pull off its wings. She loves me, she loves me not. Goneril!"

Goneril begins to play. Lear does his shambling dance, moving to one side, towards Edmund, his eyes flickering cunningly from Cornwall to Albany.

Unwaveringly the sword follows him.

Someone flops down beside Curan. Edgar stares at me brightly.

"*Bless thee from the foul fiend,*" he says in a high-pitched voice, laughing and looking at me expectantly. "*The foul fiend haunts poor Tom in the voice of a Nightingale. Croak not, black angel, I have no food for thee.*" He laughs again.

"I'm glad to see you, flesh of ice. You have led me a merry dance and run me skinny with the searching. I have searched long to scuttle my love and my secret in the ocean of your flesh. I have followed you here, lady, through worlds where I could not die."

He falls silent and gazes at my face as if he has never seen it before.

"Ah! What a perfect imitation. Those lips are Curan's exactly, the eyes perfect to a lash, the shape of the face moulded to the exact form. Curan in every detail and precision of image. Limbs, arms, the angle of the body. How well you deceive, you halflings, blessed simulacrum! Return me to dust. We all move a little closer to God. With every step. Look. Look at my hands!"

I see his hands are singed and his fingers horribly burnt, and begin to draw away.

"I burnt my hands praying, over a candle, there in the church. I felt no pain. I knew the time of miracles was upon me, if I could but read the signs and stick to the right and true path. I never lost the thread. Grimly I held on to it. I understand now that the world has only a provisional existence. Out of that provision I came and will return; and only by the sacrifice of my love will I be shed of these things."

Tears are running down his cheeks.

"So let us embrace and put an end to it. I long for your sweet kiss."

He looks at me yearningly.

Lear proceeds to rip off his clothes. Albany helps him while Cornwall keeps the sword steady. Edmund is holding Cordelia from behind, half embracing the ape, half keeping him in place.

"*An unaccommodated man* is such a bare, no, is such, no, *is but such a poor, bare, forked animal as thou.*" Lear makes as if to bow to Caliban, moving a step closer. "*O you lendings, come unbutton here.*" Albany does his bidding, pulling Lear's shirt from his back. "A man may dance and still not cry," Lear says to Albany. "If crying were meat we'd all have full stomachs. This is my song:

'My crying places are empty
My crying places are full
I pass among the people
Who feel my pitiless rule.'"

Goneril strums.

Oswald, his back to the stage, cradles Little Extra tight to his body as if she is a baby, rocking gently. The child struggles against him and climbs onto his shoulder. He tries to pull her down before she can see anything but is too late. Little Extra stares in wonderment.

The stage is full of angels.

Now that Lear is naked Albany tries to kiss him, putting his arms clumsily around his neck.

"Please, please, I know how you feel," he says in a reasonable voice. "I used to feel like that myself. It won't hurt you to be kissed, believe me. The juices of a man's mouth are as sweet as any woman's."

Lear pushes him away, his eyes on his sword. Cornwall's arm is beginning to grow tired; the tip of the sword is making ragged loops in the air.

The Fool passes Lear on his way off stage.

"*When we are born we cry that we are come
To this great stage of Fools,*" he says as he goes past.

Albany drops to his knees in front of Lear.

Lear's cock hangs at a sad angle.

Edgar wriggles closer to Curan.

"If I touched you, would my hand pass right through you, flesh of thought? When you tear out my heart, will it warm your lips a fraction?" He looks at me in sudden terror.

"*Bless thee from whirlwinds* and don't delay, angel." He reaches out and touches me.

"Flesh?" he says in wonderment. "What warm deceit! What trouble you've taken. Let me be born back into life. Come, pick the artery from my neck. *Bless your five wits.*"

He begins to undress. "It is not seemly to be born in your doublet, jerkin, hose and gown. See these patches? Climbing up my spine? The moon has rotted me there with the garbage of my time; yet by such agencies we move a little closer to God. Don't ask why God hides so; it's left to us to decode the flesh and flowers." He grinds his teeth hard, grinning at me ferociously.

"I am naked and part of the forest. *Edgar I nothing am.*" He gestures to the stage. "This is compost."

Goneril is playing but it is not an Elizabethan pastoral I hear, but the lilting melody I recognize, just too fine for the human ear. The epic of the little people. Edgar strokes my arm.

Kneeling, Albany takes Lear's cock gently into his hands. As he looks down at it, withered in his hand, his tears fall. They roll down his cheeks, onto his arms and down over his fingers onto Lear. His mouth goes wet and slippery; his sorrow becomes all-encompassing.

"*Oh let me kiss that hand,*" minces Cornwall, letting the sword fall to his side.

Albany minces in return, "*Let me wipe it first, for it smells of mortality.*"

Lear leaps, smashing the giggling Cornwall across the face, tearing the sword from the Duke's stupefied fingers. Cornwall staggers back as Lear swings towards Edmund. Albany pitches head first onto the ground.

Edmund eyes Lear warily.

"Come, nuncle, the day is late. Now is not the time for heroics or you'll lose more than your virginity." He steps away from Caliban towards Lear.

Lear swings the blade. It makes a rushing sound in the air. The world is like an eggshell, he thinks.

Edmund parries the blow with his arm, intercepting at the wrist, sending the blade spinning and Lear tumbling. Edmund goes for the sword, flourishing it at the audience with a whoop.

Lear's hands fumble for a grip. They counter something slippery and clotted. One of Gloucester's eyes. And something else. His stick with its hard, brass knob. Edmund advances, the sword dancing in front of him.

"We'll split him down the backbone and roast him with the wench," Edmund says to Cornwall. As he brings the sword down, Lear brings his stick up, cracking Edmund on the elbow. Edmund curses as the sword jabs into his own knee. He wrests it back into control, pushes Lear's arms aside and pins him down at the shoulder.

"Now you'll feel the mosquito bite, nuncle."

He thrusts the sword deep into the flesh above Lear's collar-bone. He draws it out for another strike.

"Where's the heart, nuncle?" Flicks the skin open. "About here?"

Caliban roars. Edmund swings around. The beast leaps across Cordelia to the front of the stage. It peers out into the forest beyond the audience, many of whom have shrunk into the shadows.

Edmund pursues it. Seeing him coming, the animal leaps away, bounding over the slope of the amphitheatre and into the forest.

"It has come to this," Edgar says to Curan. "Lie down in the earth." I run.

I've been a fool for too long, Gloucester thinks, stepping gingerly onto the jetty. Now the rings have fallen from my eyes and I can see. What miracle is this! Here is the barge, overburdened with flowers. Some of them fall into the river, just as Edgar has said, and are carried away by the dark water. Here's the moon, bouncing off the river. Well caught! And here's Edgar, tall and handsome, holding a stick out for me. I am whole.

"Mainchance and I are the only original members of The Shakespeare Company, Edgar, did you know that? Except the Fool. One must always except the Fool. We used to gamble, staking the treasures we'd robbed from corpses for a bit of good food. Loves his bite, does Mainchance. Once we put down fifty gold Krugerrands for a side of a pig. It was a good deal. You might not have realized, but I was called Slink in those days."

"Slink." Kent repeats, helping Gloucester onto the wharf.

"I never knew another name. I'd set up the marks for Mainchance. Sometimes we went hungry, sometimes we lived off the fat of it.

"There was a terrible Sickness upon us, in those days. There were barges on the river, piled with corpses. We had a rowboat and we'd board the barges and plunder the dead. Mainchance had never heard of Shakespeare then. Looting the dead is hard work. When we grew tired Mainchance would pull out his weed and we'd sit on top of the pile of bodies and get looped, giggling and laughing like a couple of idiots, our arms around each other's shoulders.

"Mainchance doesn't like to be reminded of those times now. He's moved into his greatness. He's forgotten his origins. He's turned his back on his old friends and talks about balance, redress and dramatic form. It's all hard work for me with no compensation. Cordelia loves me like some old uncle but doesn't come to my bed, to warm her uncle's bones. Mainchance has got it sweet now he's discovered Shakespeare. People rattle sheets of tin while he shouts and rages. The elements contend. Kent is put in the stocks. My eyes are plucked out. Bodies pile up on the stage and when messengers bring news of more it is pushed aside with a *Tis but a trifle*. Ha! I'd rather plunder barges or clean out a mark. It's safer, more honest. *Tis but a trifle*. This playing is the devil's work."

Kent leads him further out onto the jetty, past where the barge is moored. With infinite patience he works Gloucester towards the end of the jetty. He talks to the Earl softly, confirming his views and prejudices.

Gloucester looks up at the clear sky. Like him, it has been washed clean.

"They were scams, Edgar, but we knew what we were dealing with. Mainchance had a green velvet smoking jacket and could palm cards right under your nose and you'd never see it for looking. What! Ho!"

He stops.

"What's the matter?" Kent asks casually. "Another couple of steps and we'll be there."

"I know perfectly well where I am," Gloucester says with asperity. "Even a blind man can smell the river and know the rub of wood. But I don't like the look of the guard there. The one who stands by the gangplank. I can't see the face for the hood. Ask him to go away, my good angel."

"Guard!" Kent calls out in a commanding voice. "The Earl of Gloucester passes here, and seeks entrance. Stand aside!"

"He's not obeying you, Edgar," Gloucester says in panic. "I don't know if I can go on; my legs have no more strength in them."

"Move forward," Kent urges. "He will move aside for you."

Gloucester takes a tottering step forward.

"Ha!" he cries in relief. "It's only Caliban, that stupid ape. Someone has dressed him up as a monk. A pallbearer. This fancy dress must be part of the festivities."

Kent seizes on the suggestion. "That's right, Gloucester. Some silly prank. I smell the hand of Edmund in this."

"Edmund is our bastard son," Gloucester says. "And Caliban is, in the generational cycle, bastard son to Edmund."

"Well put." He pokes the weeds under Gloucester's nose again. "Can you smell the flowers?"

"Yes, yes," Gloucester pauses, considering.

"One more step," says Kent.

"This cycle dooms us to return," Gloucester says gloomily. He looks down at the dark water; a familiar, rushing face.

"Step on board, uncle, watch the gangplank," calling in a loud voice, "Prepare to receive the Duke!"

Nodding and smiling, Gloucester steps forward.

Instantly the water covers him. Kent watches for a moment, then turns around.

Curan is coming along the jetty.

Lear groans and rolls over, feeling the cold flagstones against his hip and left shoulder. He squints his eyes against the light, watching the play of colours from the stained-glass windows. Idly his eye follows the sinuous line of the tiled mosaic on the nearest pillar until it arches out of sight above him.

He groans and rolls back the other way, to the sight of Gloucester, on his hands and knees, shaking his head and trying to stand.

"I had a terrible dream," Lear says, rubbing his shoulder. "We were in some horrible cramped place. I couldn't stretch my legs properly." Wobbling, he gets to his feet.

"We performed last night," Gloucester says, touching his face.

"That's right. It was our finest performance ever." Lear draws some fresh air into his lungs and looks around him.

Most of the cast are still asleep. Nearby Cordelia lies wrapped in the arms of her hermaphrodite lover, her head resting on a cloud of hair. Lear sighs. Such beauty! A little further off Edmund is lying, his face pursed in fierce concentration, his arms wrapped tightly around his ape. Lear frowns. There's danger from that quarter, even in gracious Babylon. Curan lies at Edmund's feet, loosely in the arms of the young man with black glossy hair and lustrous skin. Lear grins.

"I think our young Courtier lost her girlhood in the night's revel." He laughs indulgently. "Such lust; it's an old witchcraft."

"Revel?" Gloucester looks down at his feet. They appear from beneath the lacy hem of satin robes.

On the other side of Curan Lear spies Regan, two slave girls draped across her limbs. Goneril lies near them, her lute perched on top of her belly. Regan appears to be asleep but she has one eyelid partly open with a part of one eye showing. The gypsy never sleeps, Lear thinks with a shiver. It's hardly natural.

Gloucester is looking dumbly at the pattern of the flagstones on the floor. He runs a finger down a joining line.

"What is this place, Mainchance?" he says it slowly.

"Babylon of course. City of cities." Lear's attention is distracted by the fountain that rises from between spaced pillars. The water, falling in a graceful arch, a fine mist passing through the stained light. There's something bobbing in the pool beneath. To get to the fountain Lear has to step over a dead bird, one of the thin, elegant legged variety that stalked unobtrusively among the guests the night before. Glancing down at the creature whose neck has been broken, Lear notices rubies and emeralds embedded in its features and crest.

Gloucester joins him.

"And by the way, Gloucester, since we're on names, you must not call me that. That I am not. I never was. We're talking trade names," he pauses to sniff at a goblet of red wine, "Do you want to be called Slink?"

"I am Slink."

Lear gestures impatiently, "Have it your own way. I am not Mainchance. That's an old calamity."

They arrive at the fountain and look into the water. Kent is lying submerged, face up, his eyes standing out from his face like two pieces of marble, his mouth gaping.

"We lost one," Lear says.

Gloucester grimaces.

Beyond them, on the other side of the fountain, Oswald lies, his knees drawn almost all the way up to his chin. Extra and Banquo's Children are near him, huddled together in sleep, Extra's thumb half in her mouth.

There are other sleepers too, the lords and ladies of Babylon. Our audience, Lear thinks with satisfaction. All are lying in postures of drunken slumber and abandon amid plates still heaped with food. In one huge platter of half eaten meat a yellow dog lies sprawled out asleep.

Lear picks up a leg of cold pork and rips off a few chunks with his teeth, chews thoughtfully.

We played them, he thinks, we played *Lear*. The lords and ladies in their fine costumes up in the galleries, the hoards in the pit, had all shifted forward in their seats. Ha ha!

"You know," chewing, "I don't fancy the chances of those stones staying very long on that dead fowl, Slink." He wipes his jaw with the back of his hand, "No, sir, those are long odds."

Gloucester cannot feel the same satisfaction. He sees this place quite differently and cannot feel at ease here. The banquet room itself is far too big. The stained glass windows glint above them like pieces of sky, and beyond that a profusion of arches and pillars bewildering to the eye. Time poised on the blurred edge of present and past.

I'm going to fall over, Gloucester thinks. There are long corridors to the floor.

"There's something not right, Mainchance," he says dubiously. He picks up a decanter of wine and fills the glass Lear has put down. When he holds it up to his face, closing with one eye and squinting with the other, and shakes the glass, the wine turns into a mass of jarring edges.

"Definitely. And I can't remember a single line from the play."

Lear chuckles. "It'll come back. By the afternoon. Have some food." He throws the bone down and turns away from the fountain.

Gloucester gestures to Kent.

"He makes an ugly fish."

Lear heads for a circle of bright sunlight, carefully stepping over the sleeping bodies. One of them, clearly a lord deep in the years of his reveling, has a face peculiarly gaunt, his skin white and flakey.

Gratefully, Lear passes between the circular doors.

"Leave these dreamers behind, Gloucester. Ah!" The sunlight hits him like a shout. In the distance it glints on the river where the *Earl of Southampton* rides, its rich canopies flapping in the light breeze; and bounces green off the tall trees that line the river bank. Behind him, the turrets and spires of Babylon. It slides down the gentle slope before him and into the river.

Gloucester emerges and stands beside him.

He follows me everywhere, Lear thinks; with a face like a hearse.

"Mainchance, when did we get here?"

Lear looks pitying at his old friend.

"Yesterday. We came up the river. You said the sunset was like a blade of flame, or words to that effect. We rehearsed in the temple and played in the palace, to royalty and its consort." He brushes the dust that glints on his jacket.

"*King Lear*, Gloucester, the greatest of the Bard's tragedies. Written somewhere between 1605 and 1606, if that's any help." He picks a piece of meat from between his teeth. "Literary historians are not exactly sure of the date."

No, as far as Gloucester is concerned, that is not very much help. There are more immediate problems than the exact dating of Shakespeare's plays. Even more immediately than the likelihood of Gloucester saying 'blade of flame'.

Of immediate priority is the sensation that this is all familiar to him. That he grew up and ran as a boy in these streets. It lies sideways to his memory.

"And after the performance, the revel. You breathed deep over many amphorae, Slink. Then pawed the slave girls," winks lewdly at Gloucester, "shuttling the red wine down your throat."

"No, no," Gloucester says, "I wasn't doing anything like that at all."

"I think life as a travelling player in The Shakespeare Company might be getting a bit much for you, Slink," Lear says dryly.

Gloucester can be so wearying.

Edgar is on the lawn exercising vigorously. First he becomes a tree, stretching for the sky with one hand and to the earth with the other. The arc between. Then he is a leaping tree, keeping his arms stretched and scissoring his legs in the air. Now he is a lion, mouth open, tongue arched towards the ground. He is a branch moving in the wind. He bounces an orange bubble on his chest. He is the wind that carves storms; the restless tide of the ocean. He stands stork-like on one leg and arches over into a bridge. The arc across. A profusion of green things grow under him. He floats on a square of purple. He pulls coloured thread from his nostrils and wraps them around his wrist. Puts his feet into the air and dives into the earth like a fish, reappears feet first and flicks back into upright. The sun rolls along his spine. Bravo! He is a wheel, all spokes and whirling hub flashing over the green. The arc through.

Bravo!

"What a way to greet the day!" Lear says exultantly. Edgar comes up beaming.

"I have found happiness here," he says to Lear.

The Fool runs up to Lear and grabs him urgently by the arm. He tries to pull Lear to one side, opening and shutting his mouth as one in great panic, looking around him, terrified.

"*Let go thy hold when a great wheel runs down a hill… This cold night will turn us all to Fools and madmen.*"

"Night?" Lear turns to Gloucester. "The Fool thinks it is night when it is clear as ever a morning."

"I've heard," says Gloucester slowly, "that what is day to the Fool is night to the wise."

"That's fool enough," Lear says, "to put out the sun. Or rise in the evening."

"*And I'll go to bed at noon,*" the Fool says.

Lear shakes the Fool off. Here is one who has become lost in the play, looking out only from its lines. He must really be a fool to do something like that.

"*Reason is madness,*" Edgar says to Lear, still smiling radiantly.

"That's right," says Lear, getting into the spirit of it, slapping one fist into his palm.

"*… What, prisoner?*

I am the natural fool of fortune, use me well… "

Lear turns to Edgar.

"*I'll talk a word with this same learned Thebean.*"

"Then hear my words," Edgar says loftily. "All the way upriver I have been looking for a home. A place to get off and leave the river behind me. You're not the only one who's plied the boats. I wandered in the nothing;

199

the horizontal place between ports. I dreamed of tunnels. I was shown the key to transformations. Now I'm here all that is finished with. There is just the ongoing moment precipitate." He lifts his hands to the air and rolls a spectrum out from his skull to either side of his body.

"To begin with I lusted after the flesh. Curan to be exact; yes," holds palms up, "I lusted after Curan. That fell away and the body was renewed." Proudly he looks down at his fit, handsome body.

"Frankly, I couldn't have asked for more. I don't even deserve it."

"I myself have lusted after Curan," Lear says testily, offended by the unctuous tone that has crept into Edgar's voice. "Everyone has at one time or another. It's an occupational hazard. I don't see it's all that remarkable," he scratches his sore shoulder. "Not worth losing your heart."

Edgar nods his head devoutly. "Oh yes, yes, very much worth losing your heart." Pinpricks of light explode in the air as he laughs.

"Can the heart be taken from the body and still live, king?"

Cordelia runs up to them. She is naked and her body gleams with pearls of water. Her face and skin are glowing. She pulls impulsively at Lear's arm.

"There's a fountain, in the gardens. White roses float on the water. It's beautifully chill. You can dive for jewels there. Come and swim, my love; learn to play the dolphin!"

"I will. Later…" Lear is obscurely annoyed by the turn of events.

"I didn't know what contentment was," Edgar says to Cordelia. "My mind swung fearfully from one thing to another. I suffered crushing burdens, murderous divisions, death fantasies. I held my hand over a flame; it did not touch my flesh but roasted the kernel of my heart. I embraced a woman of fire and was made over into this substance. Listen:

'When the cage of the five coloured swan
was shattered, the bee fell
to the ground with wings broken.'"

Cordelia curtseys gracefully. Her hair fans the sunlight.

"My mind was as restless as Edmund's ape. I flew with angels and gibbered with the dead. None of that is necessary now. I am here in Babylon, and when the Company moves on I will stay." He glances at Lear. "Do you understand, king?"

Lear turns away. There are always problems with Edgar, yet he somehow manages to get on stage for his lines. He'll face Edgar later. Right now he needs time to breathe the clean fresh air. To wander into the rose gardens, perhaps, and sit for a while. Take a little time to enjoy paradise.

"Are we going to play here again tonight?" Gloucester asks him.

Edmund joins them, leading Caliban on a leash. He won't look at any of them but keeps his eyes firmly on the ground, a surly look on his face. No greetings from the Bastard, Lear thinks wryly.

"The Bastard Son looks like he's been treading on tacks this morning," Lear observes.

"Perhaps you'd like to swim in the fountain," Cordelia says brightly to Edmund, drops of water still glistening on her shoulders and breasts.

His eyes travel up and over her nakedness.

"No, I don't think so." He meets her gaze arrogantly. Caliban pulls loose and runs over to Cordelia, trying to jerk his crotch up against her. Cordelia pushes him away, laughing easily.

"Caliban!" Edmund screams hoarsely. He aims a vicious kick for the animal's flanks. Caliban dances back, easily evading it.

"I've seen dogs that try to do that all the time," says Gloucester.

Edgar turns to Edmund.

"I've found a home for the body," he says.

"Good for you," Edmund says. "You'd best bury it before it starts to go rank."

"Look at what I've found to match your brooch," Cordelia says to Lear. She holds her hand forward and like a conjurer opens her palm. An opal gleams in the sun. "I'll get the forges here in Babylon to cast you a ring of pure gold."

Lear looks at the stone humbly.

"I'm in the shadow of your love," he says quietly.

"I'll never leave here," Edgar says to Edmund.

"*The prince of darkness is a gentleman; Modo he's called, and Mahu,*" the Fool says to Edgar.

Lear claps his hands. "Wake up some slaves! Ho! We need food. We'll breakfast here on the lawn."

Reflexively, Edmund shakes the pocket of his shirt. There is a reassuring rattle. Cornwall and Albany approach him. Albany is smiling.

"This place is full of sodomites," Cornwall says in disgust.

Albany puts his hand to his mouth. "Don't tell Edmund. He'll put them all to the sword."

Edmund takes out his tin and opens it. He is about to pop something into his mouth when he looks again, closer this time. His tin is filled with small stones.

"Won't you, Edmund?" Albany says insistently. He is smiling.

Curan approaches, hand in hand with the ebony youth.

"I believe our Curan has found love," Cordelia says teasingly.

Curan blushes. I can never stop myself.

"He's a handsome brute," Cornwall says. "He's probably a sodomite."

"My friend has no name," Curan says shyly.

"*Modo he's called, and Mahu,*" the Fool says to her.

"Can we find a place in the Company for him? I know he will learn fast. He's already picked up some lines. Listen."

In a light, pleasant baritone the youth says,

" ... *Welcome, then*

Thou insubstantial air that I embrace."

"Very good, very good. We might make a player of him. Groom an Othello for the cast."

"*This is the foul fiend flibbertigibbet: he begins at Curfew and walks to the first cock,*" the Fool says to Lear.

"Don't mind the Fool," Lear says to Curan. "He thinks it is night." He turns to the youth. "We'll call you Herald in the meantime, although I have the role of Kent to fill." He breaks off vaguely. There are decisions to make.

"Is Babylon your home?" Edgar asks the youth.

"I was born here, a slave in the provinces. Once a year the Lord and his Lady would pass through, choosing slaves for the palace." He bows respectfully. "I was chosen by the Lady and brought here. Curan has interceded for me and won my freedom."

Curan blushes again. Her fingers tremble as she strokes his arm.

"Step on a crack, you marry a rat," Edmund says to her.

"It fills my heart with joy to see that love has touched you," Cordelia says to Curan warmly. Curan tries to meet the golden flare of the woman's nakedness.

"Madam, it is always you I have loved," she answers boldly.

Cordelia turns to Gloucester.

"What of you, uncle? Do you want to dive into the crystal water, or would you prefer a massage?"

Lear wanders away from the table. His early exuberance has evaporated like mist from the river. His mood is curiously flat for the roundness of the morning. Surely it is Edgar who has upset him with his showing off. He looks at Gloucester's stricken face.

He feels it too, Lear thinks.

Edgar turns to Edmund. "You are grinding your teeth a lot, Edmund. I used to do that when I was a child." He takes the sunlight and bends it through his fingers. "It's a very ancient response. A teeth-sharpening exercise."

Lear finds himself returning to the pavillion where they have spent the night. Gloucester follows him. Why doesn't Gloucester go and have a look at the rose garden? Lear takes a sudden detour through part of the garden to shake Gloucester off. Flowers peddle their blank faces rapidly by.

Coming to a junction, he finds a gnome carved of granite placed at the foot of a tree. The gnome glares at him as he goes past.

"Look! Lear!"

Lear turns reluctantly. Gloucester gestures to the gnome.

"It's Kent!"

Lear passes through the circular door and into the comparative gloom of the pavilion. Most of the sleeping figures are gone.

A crying is coming from one of the pillars. A huddled figure lying on the cushions, shaking uncontrollably. Another, more bulky figure stoops down.

"She is bereft," Goneril announces as Lear approaches, Gloucester shadowing behind.

"Her people ceased to pass this way a long time ago. She fears they are gone forever; that she is the only one of them left. Try to imagine how that must feel."

"We all share a common humanity," Lear says placatingly.

"Except those whose mouths move without the knowledge of their brains," Goneril snaps.

Regan raises herself brokenly from the pillows.

"Last night when the applause was at its greatest and I had drunk my fill of the sound, I heard the wind knocking on the canvas walls. I had two levels of hearing; one to hear the applause and one to hear the canvas, flap flap, flap flap." She lurches onto her feet, holding onto Regan and Lear for support. "When I tried to look out, beyond the lights to the audience, I couldn't find my horizons. The blood was racing through my veins but I was as cold as ice."

She retches, finishing with a loud, rasping burp.

"I felt as if I was going to fall over."

Gloucester nods his head. "Yes," he says, "Yes."

"Nothing could warm me, no flesh touch me, no vision enter me; I could no longer hear the epic of the little people, nor the songs that gust out of the moon."

"Applause is silence, clapping. No past. 'No play,'" she staggers forward, vomiting out over the flagstones, "No race, no history, no location, no geography, no arteries, no king, no ancestors…" She vomits again, choking the last bit of green bile out of her throat, coughing with a barking sound.

"It's a trap!" she shouts wildly.

Goneril thumps her on the back, humming strongly.

"And they went on clapping. Row after row. Kent was throwing tomatoes at someone in the pit. The air was filled with flies. Help! I can't hold onto them!" She staggers, sideways, reaching out to Goneril for support.

"I've got nothing more to spew," she retches. "Goneril gets pregnant, I get the nausea," she shoots the other woman a venomous look. "The creature inside her is mine."

Forgetting the two men she leans heavily on Goneril's shoulder and stares into her face.

"You have always known, witch, that my womb is sterile; now know that a few hundred or thousand miles from here the last community of gypsies died. The flame has flickered and gone out. With it goes my colour and substance."

"Regan will live, but the gypsy inside her is dying of grief," Goneril says, almost accusing the two men. "She's psychically sensitive. She becomes a focus, a lightning rod for all kinds of," she rolls her eyes mysteriously upwards, "influences."

Lear glances over at Gloucester whose eyes are fixed eagerly on Regan. So these are the kind of people I have to turn into a Company, to get on the stage at the end of the day. Good grief, heart of mine: who would be Lear?

He draws himself up to his full height.

"I don't think anyone has any need to feel let down after last night's performance," he says loftily. "We played well, we…" He is caught by Goneril's rigid stare.

"You don't know anything about it," she says emphatically. "It's true of all men. In general. And you in particular. Not a bloody clue."

"My tears will cut my eyes to pieces," Regan says.

"Which is the fate of widows," Goneril says fiercely. "In this case the bridegroom turned up wearing a bare jawbone and ribs to play songs in the wind. Would you stand in line, Lord, for his granite kiss?"

"Edmund has a bird living inside his chest cavity," Regan says tonelessly. "A horrible thing. A parasite. It actually lives there, displacing his own tissue, taking over the function of his internal organs." Regan looks at them all bleakly.

"None of us will leave this place," she says with an air of finality.

Gloucester nods in melancholic agreement.

"None of us," he repeats.

Lear heads for the door, half in flight, half in royal exit. Regan has a bad dream so the rest of the cast must go mad. Their conversation could go on forever.

Gratefully he passes out into the sunlight once more. He can feel the warmth of it soaking into his skin. The earth tips forward along its ancient curve.

The cast are still on the lawn, enjoying the morning. Extra is in conversation with Curan, both girls giggling, Extra's eyes straying, every now and then, to the smiling Herald. Little Extra has taken off her clothes and is running naked like Cordelia; her body glossy with water. They are teasing Fleance who runs for the protection of Oswald.

"I agree," Cornwall says to Edgar. "You see yourself in entirely new terms. A new context. That's your privilege. But to me, you're just the same old Edgar."

Cordelia swings Little Extra around. Wheeeeee!

Albany smiles and nods politely to Edmund.

Goneril, Regan and Gloucester join the group. Goneril is pontificating to Gloucester.

"I think we're some sort of corporate being, in some partial or incomplete state."

"Perhaps you're talking about the play," Gloucester ventures.

Extra is talking seriously to Herald, who is listening attentively. Lear takes Curan aside.

"I'm going to need a new Kent."

The Fool grabs Edgar and gestures to Lear:

"*This is not Lear...*
Does Lear walk thus? Speak thus?
Where are his eyes?
Either his notion weakens, his discernings
Are lethargied."

Gloucester nods thoughtfully at Goneril.

"I can't remember a line from the play," he says. The Fool swings around to him.

"*No further, sir; a man may rot even here,*" the Fool says to him.

"That's it," says Gloucester. "The first line to come to me; and it's my last line."

"*And that's true too,*" the Fool says.

Cordelia hugs Little Extra to her, swinging her around. The sun blazes out from their shoulders.

Edmund stares sullenly at Regan. Her hands tremble.

Edgar does a headstand, balancing the sun on his toes.

Lear's gaze sweeps behind him. The tower that rises up is a tower of water. Its vague, slim outlines are veiled in pale torrents that fall as straight as rain down over the hidden walls. From there he looks across the river to a huddle of huts and a jetty. As he sights it, that piece of the shoreline slips into an indeterminate grey. Too slippery for the eye.

> *"Thou has spoken right, 'tis true;*
> *The wheel is come full circle; I am here,"*

the Fool says quietly, his voice cracked, encrusted with time.

Lear pulls himself up to full height. *Every inch a king.*

The cast assembled.

He brings his stick down hard onto the ground.

"Rehearsal!"

There's Babylon! A few shacks and a jetty slipping away into the grey dawn as the *Earl of Southampton* drifts slowly out onto the river.

It gets smaller. The mist woollies it over in grey, its special twilight.

The jetty is empty.

Edmund stares at it morosely from the wheelhouse. He is master now. We examine him covertly. The wound in his knee, caused by Lear deflecting his blow, and the ugly bite in his neck, are clearly giving him trouble. I pray they will turn septic, or open him to the Sickness. When he walks it is with a limp, and a grimace of pain.

Now he must play Lear.

Worse than the wounds is the loss of Caliban. For the whole night to the first cheerless waxing of grey he searched the forest through, screaming the animal's name at the top of his lungs.

Edmund has lost his pet. His silence is grief and bitterness. He's either staring moodily out at the river or breaking out into some violence.

But Edmund is boss. Sometimes he grins his old Edmund grin and sings loudly.

"Alive alive-ho. Alive alive-ho!"

Cordelia comes when he calls and sits at his feet; her face sullen, movements listless. Sometimes she catches my eye and behind the varnished look I catch comprehension and complicity. We will murder Edmund. We shall wash our hands in his blood.

Edmund is joined by Kent, who squats on the roof of the wheelhouse. He has gone up in the world, has Kent the dwarf. He's been promoted. With Edmund playing Lear, Kent slots into Edmund's role; an astute choice by Edmund. With Kent here as Edmund, his flank is covered.

When Kent sees Curan his eyes narrow. There will be time for Curan later.

"It's only for tonight," Edmund tells him. "Until I decide what we're going to do." After the next village.

Lear is lying in the quarters below. Since being wounded he has gone into a delirium. Oswald and Cordelia take turns at watching over him. Oswald says it is not the Sickness, as we understand it, but plain river fever. We all fear, though, what we hope for Edmund: that the wound, in this case the shoulder, has become infected.

Edmund has given him the role of Gloucester, but it is doubtful that he will be playing it, tonight at least. There is a white film over his eyes.

"Gloucester can never come in exactly on cue," he babbles to Oswald and Little Extra, "he is always fractionally late. Have you noticed that?"

Curan makes her way to the front of the barge, weathering the lizard stare of the dwarf. Regan will be waiting for me in the wheelhouse, where Cordelia used to stand gazing out over the river.

There are big changes in the women's roles. Since Goneril is too near term to go on acting Regan will take her part. I'm to be moved to Regan's part.

Me, Regan!

When she heard the news she gave me a silky grin. She says that Goneril is the true villain of the play and that the role offers her more scope.

Extra is pleased for she is to be moved into Kent's role, even though she's a girl. When I congratulated her she poked her tongue out at me.

It embarrasses me to remember what I used to do with her.

Banquo's Children are no more. Little Extra never leaves Oswald's side, while Fleance has attached himself to Edmund, swaggering the way Edmund does, wearing his shirt open at the front and grinning at people. Extra is all sulky and will hardly talk to anyone.

Fleance will play Curan. There are two new Extras to fill the minor roles, I have to pass them on my way to the front of the barge. It is the tawny-haired girl and her companion from the previous night's audience.

Edmund, in a flash of his old style, dragged them squealing from one of the shacks at dawn, kicking his way through the walls as he departed, turning them into a cyclone of tin and wood.

The girl won't give us her name, or hasn't got one, so we're calling her Herald and the boy France. As I pass Herald looks up with fear and respect.

"That's Regan," she whispers to France.

I remember her eyes riveted upon me last night. Boldly, I meet her stare.

Before reaching the wheelhouse I have to skirt around Edgar who sits on the deck nursing his bandaged hands. He mutters to himself and sometimes talks out loud to invisible beings just as poor Tom does in the play. He has tried to tell everyone that Gloucester was taken by strange creatures that make raids on us from another reality. A mutant reality.

But nobody listens to Edgar now that the marks of the Sickness are upon his face and his dark secret is known to us all. Edmund is certainly not interested in Edgar's theories; to him they are simply another manifestation of the Sickness and he has forbidden Oswald, Edgar and Little Extra the use of the living quarters below. At nights they will huddle beneath a tarpaulin stretched across the deck.

I avoid looking at Edgar. He scares me, scares me more than Edmund does. *The foul fiend haunts poor Tom in the voice of a nightingale.*

Regan steps out from the shadow of the wheelhouse, sleek and feline. Here is the real source of Edmund's power. Her fingers float up to my face and lightly touch my cheek. They are smooth and utterly white with bright red fingernails. I will go to her bed tonight. I'll wriggle like a worm into her body.

Finally I reach the front of the boat. There is a small expanse here; just the right size for me to lie. I can look back and see most of the cast. This is the last time I will see them as Curan. I may sleep, and when I awake the world will be different.

I want to see them as if I have never seen them before. I want to see them as the dawn washes the paint off their faces. I want to see them unmasked.

Looking at them like this I realize with a shock none is very old at all. Even Lear, down on his bed of pain. Even poor departed Gloucester.

Lear can be no more than three or four years older than Curan. Cordelia and Regan even younger than Lear. Regan must have been lying when she accused Cordelia and Lear of incest. Unless they are brother and sister.

We are just children of the river. Phantom barges pass, loaded with corpses.

Curan has seen enough of it. There is a cold weariness in her bones. The air is flat and damp. She lies with her back on the deck, closes her eyes and allows the comfortable dark to settle in around her. She can hear the gentle curve of the wave peeling back from the bow. She can also hear the hectoring voices of Cornwall and Albany, finally awake and about to pester Edmund for the day's first pills.

Now Curan, she reprimands, you are going to forget them. When you open your eyes they will still be there. In the meantime, let the river carry their voices away, like rags in the wind.

When you open your eyes they will still be there. There is a brute certainty in what they are. You can relax and they will sustain their existence, fulfill their commission, without your intervention or even acknowledgement.

You can relax and let them pass. Adjust your breathing. In. Out. In. Out.

You can change it all. You can let the sky breathe into your lungs.

In. Out. With all you have been holding in the frail vessel of a body, break up and yield to the act of breathing. No Babylon but the spacey dark behind the eyes. Lear and his train are there (fifty retainers, a hundred), leave them their footprints upon the moon.

Your rib-cage is falling, down, filling your body cavity with air. In. Out.

She is growing. Her hands are as tiny as ants, folded across her stomach. The river runs through her limbs; her head swallows the boat; the ocean pours into her eyes.

She fills out the whole space with air. In. In. In. Then she expels it in a long parabola of breath. Out. Out. Out.

'Til there is not a particle or dream of absence left. In. In. In.

Her breathing becomes an undulating wave front of breaths, stamped with her special curve and frequency.

She visualizes the ocean and watches the tide wash back and forth along her spine.

She visualizes the earth and feels it take root in the tailbone.

She visualizes the wind, soaring through the empty dark of her flesh.

She visualizes fire that leaps the throat and scatters along the veins.

She is the steady breathing of space. In through the nose and out through the feet.

In. Out.

A thick porridgy substance flows out of her mouth and onto the deck. It is yellow, with more viscosity than mucous.

She goes on breathing, steadily, regularly, with the reflex of rib and tendon.

In.

Out.

Each age its time and face location.

In.

Out.

She pulls more of the yellowy substance out of her mouth, unraveling it in long threads. Her breathing becomes easier, more fluid. Her visualizations slip into one another as she loops each golden arc between breaths. In. Out.

She is big enough to contain the whole universe. To hold it within her. To bring it to an end.

To transmute it within her substance to something new. Something different.

Cordelia, arms outstretched, face of joy.

In through the nose and out through the feet.

In through the nose and out through the feet.

In through the nose and out through the feet.

Breath of breath

We can heal, even here

Let it go

A cool wind blows off the river.

ACKNOWLEDGEMENTS

Textual quotes, apart from Shakespeare's King Lear, which are all in italics, are from Sappho, Allama Prabhu, Thomas Campion, Robert Jones, William Corkine and Anton Dvorak.

Many thanks to Leila Lees, who lived with it as it grew; Warwick Jordan, who first put it out into the world; Tony Beyer, Biddy Hamilton and Tom Frewen, who worked on it; Lindsay Rabbitt and Jane Poutney, for their unflagging support; the members of the N.Z. Literary Fund Advisory Committee, who backed it; and for Phil Dick, who would have liked it.

Thanks to Jennifer Rackham for cover design; Odette Singleton-Wards (Eagle Eye Odey) for proofreading; and Mahina Marshall for interior design and project management.

The Fool by Hans Holbein

Also by Mike Johnson

Novels
Lethal Dose
Zombie in a Spacesuit
Hold My Teeth While I Teach You to Dance
Travesty
Counterpart
Stench
Dumbshow
Antibody Positive
Lear: The Shakespeare Company Plays Lear at Babylon

Shorter Fiction
Confessions of a Cockroach/Headstone
Back in the Day: Tales of NZ's Own Paradise Island
Foreigners

Poetry
The Raising Light Trilogy
Ladder With No Rungs, Illustrated by Leila Lees
Two Lines and a Garden, Illustrated by Leila Lees
To Beatrice: Where We Crossed the Line
Vertical Harp: The Selected Poems of Li He
Treasure Hunt
Standing Wave
From a Woman in Mt Eden Prison & Drawing Lessons
The Palanquin Ropes

Non-Fiction
Angel of Compassion

Children's Fiction
Kenni and the Roof Slide, Illustrated by Jennifer Rackham
Taniwha. Illustrated by Jennifer Rackham

www.ingramcontent.com/pod-product-compliance
Lightning Source LLC
Chambersburg PA
CBHW020613300426
44113CB00007B/619